My Dearest,
You were my chosen one; you chose no.
That is as it should be;
All is well;
G-d's will be done.

As Jacob wrestled with G-d and won,
so does an alcoholic
wrestle with their addiction.
They do not, however, always win.

Other works by Cris Robins
Finding Grace – a Journey of Self-Discovery
The Not Perfect But Better Diet
Stories to Sleep to (a CD)

My Dearest Jacob:
Letters to a closet alcoholic

Riverhouse Publishing
St. Louis MO 63146
ISBN: 1-893892-04-2

DEDICATION

It needs to be said first, that without G-d and His patience and His wonderful sense of humor, this work would have just been one of the many thoughts swimming around in my head that never went anywhere. This is another gift to Him.

This book is also dedicated not to the alcoholics, but to the ones who love them; put up with them; fear for them; and have the courage to stay with them.

This is to show those people that it really isn't them; and perhaps to show the alcoholic what it's like to live with them. If you think this work is a roller-coaster ride, a series of contradictions, a mish-mash of comings and goings; you're right.

I know of no better way to illustrate the madness of loving an alcoholic than to show it this way.

A NOTE FROM THE AUTHOR

Dear Reader,

There are times in our lives when we think we are going stark-raving mad; when we look about us and nothing is working.

If you are in love with an alcoholic, closet or not, dry drunk or active, you may be able to relate to this insanity; the ups and downs; the lies and betrayals; the selfishness of the other party.

And you may think this is your fault; that you are somehow responsible for the other's actions; that you are the cause of this; and that if you ... changed ... one ... more ... thing ... all would be well.

I'm here to tell you; it has very little to do with you. There is nothing you can say, or do, or not say, or not do to make the other person change their ways, to stop their drinking, to make them love you, or need you, or want you the way that you love them, and need them, and want them to.

It has been my experience that it doesn't work that way. There is no magic wand, no sacred prayer, or no fairy dust that will make this relationship all better just because you want it to be better. What there is, however, is your ability to survive; your choice to change; and your chance to make *you* better.

I know what it's like to love another so very completely and have them discount and disregard all that you are and want to give them. I know what it's like to love some one so deeply that you are willing to believe the lies time and time and time again. I also know the pain of them leaving without so much as a good bye, for reasons I still don't understand.

This work is my Twelfth Step contribution; my passing on of the message to others. Hopefully this will ease your pain, calm your doubts, and let you know you are NOT alone. May you walk your journey knowing you are loved.

With grace,
Cris

THE TWELVE STEPS OF ALCOHOLICS ANONYMOUS

1. We admitted we were powerless over alcohol—that our lives had become unmanageable.
2. Came to believe that a Power greater than ourselves could restore us to sanity.
3. Made a decision to turn our will and our lives over to the care of God *as we understood Him.*
4. Made a searching and fearless moral inventory of ourselves.
5. Admitted to God, to ourselves, and to another human being the exact nature of our wrongs.
6. Were entirely ready to have God remove all these defects of character.
7. Humbly asked Him to remove our shortcomings.
8. Made a list of all persons we had harmed, and became willing to make amends to them all.
9. Made direct amends to such people wherever possible, except when to do so would injure them or others.
10. Continued to take personal inventory and when we were wrong promptly admitted it.
11. Sought through prayer and meditation to improve our conscious contact with God, *as we understood Him*, praying only for knowledge of His will for us and the power to carry that out.
12. Having had a spiritual awakening as the result of these Steps, we tried to carry this message to alcoholics, and to practice these principles in all our affairs.

TABLE OF CONTENTS

INTRODUCTION

Insanity. There, I said it. That's the one word loving an alcoholic exemplifies. Going in the same circles; hearing the same lies; living the same situations ... over, and over, and over again.

Nothing changes; sure the days turn into weeks; and the weeks into months; and the months into years; and the lies may be different ... but everything is still ... the same. Time passes and until YOU change, the cycle will still continue; or, it could get ... worse.

If you think this work is about how to get your loved one to stop drinking, it isn't. What it is about is showing you the insanity I lived through; yes, it could have been much worse than it was. But did it really need to be? I don't think so.

I've written this book to follow a calendar year, divided into 12 sections, each one based on one of the 12 steps of recovery from Alcoholics Anonymous. The book will actually begin in February. However, the cycle can be started in any month.

It's also about how the 12 steps of AA recovery mirrored our relationship ... not HIS recovery, but mine. Each section will list the step of that month; and will contain several different writings, with some fill-in-the-blanks of what wasn't said to round out the section as needed. It is my hope that there will be a story to the words, not just the words.

At the end of each section there will be a place for you to think, and write, and maybe even relate. The purpose of the monthly summary is to help you assess any situation that may be hampering your relationship. You are encouraged to use the blank space provided to find your own method of dealing with the issue.

As for me, I didn't say goodbye to him; I was willing to continue the cycle of anger, hurt, and betrayal, as the bond between us was that strong ... mine for him, not the other way around. I am grateful that he left; grateful that I've been able to spend this time processing all that happened. It is my hope that you will grow stronger, strong enough to realize you can leave the relationship or you can stay. Either way, my hope is you will be strong enough to make the decision that is right ... for you.

February

Step 1

We admitted we were powerless over alcohol -- that our lives had become unmanageable.

~ *Alcoholics Anonymous*

IN THE BEGINNING ...

My Dearest Jacob,

When can I come home?

I love you, too.

C

~~

I said them; the same words he'd said to me just a few days ago. How was it possible for my life to be turned upside down and inside out in just six days?? How could I have gone from a strong, independent, woman to some sniveling jelly fish in such a very short time?

I didn't know, but I didn't like it. Let's recap:

Saturday: Arguing with now-ex boyfriend. I get an email from a stranger saying we need to talk. I ask why. He says because he is everything I've ever wanted. I laugh. I send him back an email asking what makes him think so. He says he's IT. The emails were rapid fire to the point where I finally give him my number; he sends me his picture and calls before I can walk the five feet from my computer to the closet.

We talk for over four hours and when he breaks out in song, I cry. I fell in love with him in that instant. I felt that I had suddenly known him for years; we talk the same language; we laugh at the same jokes; we just ... fit.

Sunday: We agree to meet for coffee. We do, and it just feels so right. We end up in my car and he kisses me for the first time. I whisper ... "Wow!" and ask for another; he complies saying I can have as many as I want. That's when I begin to love him. We go our separate ways. I decide to meet up with my current boyfriend to break it off with him. I do, and the new guy comes over ... and stays the night.

He tells me he loves me; that he wants something real; that I'm it for him. It's a first for me; I'd never had a man stay the night before. I like it, a lot.

Monday: I wake up with him beside me. The morning after is really good. He says he'll call. He does; we make plans for me to go to dinner at his house.

Tuesday: I go to dinner; it's very nice. I stay the night. It's even better.

Wednesday: I wake up with him. I can think of no other place on earth where I'd rather be.

Thursday, Friday, Saturday; I delete all the contact information from all the other men I've known to this point. And I sit, and I wait, and the return call doesn't come ... until the following Wednesday.

I am a smart girl; but the connection was so very strong, and he said all the right words. How could I not believe him?

How could I ever had known he was ... drunk. He didn't remember telling me all the things that he had said; he didn't remember half of the things we'd done. He only knew one thing ... I was the clingy bitch he'd slept with and he did not want a relationship ... with me.

Was I clingy? I didn't think so. I'd sent him one email in the course of a week and left him one message. I wrote him off ... until he called on Wednesday; it was really late. He said he missed me, he needed me, he wanted me. I let him come over and stay the night ... again.

It was the beginning ... of the pain and the anger and the nastiness that became my life.

But, I saw all the right signs; all the markers that the right hand of G-d was behind this – so I went, and it hurt, but the good times were so very good; until they weren't.

A BRAND NEW DAY

Today is a brand new day.

I've had five of them in my lifetime.

It is said that *every* day is a brand new day; I disagree as most days are exactly the same as the day before. Sure there may be some distinguishing differences between a weekday and a weekend; but overall most days are about the same stuff as they were the day before or the day before that one.

Then every once in a while you realize that TODAY really is different from yesterday and all the yesterdays that came before it and because it is different, nothing will ever be the same again. These are the days when you wake up and look around you, at your environment, at the life change that has just happened and realize, yes, this is good.

As I said, I've had five of these brand new days; the day after my oldest son was born; the day after my youngest son was born; the day I got my first office; the day I woke up in my first apartment; and, well, today. In each incident I found myself enjoying the morning in the new environment, much as I am right now, and I realized – nothing will ever be the same again. There are some lines that once crossed, you can't uncross. There are some changes that once made, can't be unmade; and every day will be different, because *you* are different.

And today is about as different as any day could possibly be.

As I write this I'm sitting on the floor of Jacob's living room, my lap top is comfortably sitting on the step up to his office; I'm in my pajamas and am in no hurry to get dressed. Beside me I've a cup of quickly getting cold *black* chocolate flavored coffee (as opposed to my sugared and creamed French Vanilla fare), my satchel, and my socks from last night. Of course I've my trusty cell phone, steno pad, and mints to the other side of my screen. I'm sitting close to the double-doors which lead out onto the deck; the same door that when I need a cigarette I slide back, open, and sit in the threshold to have. There's no smoking in his house and for good reason. If it were my house I wouldn't let anyone smoke in here either; it's much too nice to be disrespected in that way.

I don't HAVE to sit here; the house is big enough for me to sit in a dozen different places; and empty enough to make my own spot; but the view of the cloudy day, the birds, and the trees is so nice that the fact that there is an electrical outlet not but three feet away is just an added bonus.

He's still in bed sleeping, the house is quiet; I can hear his soft breathing, the low hum of the furnace kicking in, and the clock on his desk ticking. The din of the cars on the distant highway sound just like the rush of the ocean. These are comforts to me. There are a lot of comforts to me here, oddly enough at that. There are few places in my life that I can go without sneezing or coughing at the dust or strange smells; this isn't one of them. My first thought upon entering his home was: *home*. It felt like I'd been away somewhere and was just now returning home. Odd for a place I'd never been to with a man I barely knew; but somehow it just felt *right*. I've never spent the night with anyone I wasn't related to, so this wasn't something I did on a whim. Of course, I'd had other offers before, but I didn't feel … safe with *them*; I didn't trust *them*; and I wasn't ready to take that step with *them*.

I'd like to say that we've known each for a very long time and my spending the night at his house was just the natural progression of things; but I can't. Fact of the matter is I've cigarettes that are older than our relationship. So, why is it then, last night as we sat about watching television, talking quietly or saying nothing, it felt like we were one of those couples who had learned where each other's space was and when it was welcomed to invade it? I don't know.

I knew there was something on his mind; had been since I arrived; but, I also knew whatever it was, had nothing to do with me; he proved this as every time I'd walk away, he'd follow me. I was trying to let him have his space and he was pulling me in. I had tried to broach the subject gently, but met with resistance. So, I backed away; not with anger or hurt or animosity; but with compassion, kindness, and patience. This was new for me, a good new at that. When he was ready, I listened; and little by little he walked himself through the issue and I found that I could help by just listening, adding comments when I felt them necessary, asking questions to clarify, and just being there for him.

It felt good to be there – it was comfortable to be in his home, his arms, his thought processes. There is a certain fit, a rightness, a something-was-missing-now-it's-not to this whole situation. It seems

Step 1

I'm entering a whole new stage in the relationship arena and it's changed me, somehow.

All the things I thought I knew about relationships don't apply to this one; there are no games, there are no hoops to jump through, there is no changing my life around to meet someone else's expectations. It's just him and me; and no body else. It's making an investment in the relationship and getting a strong return on our investments every day. And, it's easy – there's no work, no issues, no problems; just taking things as they come and working them out as they happen. It's being straight up with each other; it's taking the possibility of risking the relationship to make it stronger; letting them know you've got their back; and working so that the success of one is the success of the other.

Yep, today is a brand new day and nothing will be the same for me.

NO MORE BOYFRIENDS

I'll never have another boyfriend again.

It's true, really, it is.

That is not a bitter statement of a jaded woman who's been on the receiving end of one too many "Dear Jane" e-mails; no this proclamation was the conclusion of meeting the right man, at the right time, when I was finally ready for him, and realizing the difference between "Boyfriend" and "Partner".

I came to this realization this morning shortly after 7 a.m. as I sat on my parlor bed having the first of too many cigarettes of the day and watching Jacob softly dozing in my bed. The night before he had casually stated, "I've broken down a lot of your barriers." Broken down? How about smashed to smithereens?

It wasn't enough that he was the first man to make love to me in MY bed; but that he actually STAYED the night was right up there with Congress passing a balanced budget – it just wasn't done. Period. No questions; no discussions; no wiggle room; I did NOT have *boyfriends* sleep over in my apartment. Yes, they may leave at three in the morning; but, they will be gone before the sun rises.

So why was it that not only did he stay the night – but – I asked him too? He offered to leave, he gave me that option, he told me it was my choice; and it was. Being given the choice, I asked him to stay.

Why? Because Jacob WASN'T a *boyfriend*; he was something much, much more.

As I sat on my parlor bed, the sun just barely lighting the room, I started comparing him to the other men I'd known; the things he said, the topics we discussed, and the positions he took on matters of relationships. It was through this comparison that the chasm between "Boyfriend" and "Partner" became crystal clear.

- A boyfriend opens the car door; a partner opens the mayo jar.
- A boyfriend looks good on your arm; a partner looks good talking to the mechanic about the "funny" noise under the hood.
- A boyfriend brings flowers; a partner brings the case of water up three flights of stairs.

- A boyfriend talks about all the things you need to change about you to fit into his life; a partner just 'fits'.
- A boyfriend asks if you purchased the tickets to the concert this weekend; a partner asked if you've put the bonus check in the IRA account.
- A boyfriend suggests you wile away the Monday morning in bed; a partner hustles around to leave early so you can get your work done.
- A boyfriend has your cell number; a partner has your back.
- A boyfriend is gone once the thrill is over; a partner knows that new thrills are just around the corner for the taking.
- A boyfriend talks about building a friendship; a partner talks about building a life.
- A boyfriend needs the approval of all his friends and family members to continue seeing you; a partner knows they will love you because he does, and if they don't – it's their loss.
- A boyfriend's time line is until Wednesday; a partner is forever.
- And maybe most importantly of all, a boyfriend talks about providing the beer for the party Saturday night; and a partner talks about providing a sanctuary where all the worries of the world are locked outside.

In the time it takes to smoke one cigarette I realized something that really rocked my world; it wasn't so much that the former men in my life were such lousy boyfriends; it was more because I was such a lousy *girlfriend*. I was married for over 30 years; I grew into adulthood being a wife and mother; I learned how to take care of relationships and others. I never really learned how to BE a girlfriend. I don't play girl games; I don't lie or bat my eyelashes to get my own way; and I certainly don't put up false hoops for the man in my life to jump through.

Yep, as the sun came into clear view so did my life. I am a lousy girlfriend; but, I am a GREAT partner, and it took one to show me I *am* one. I'm good with that trade off.

OVERWHELMING

Asking the Almighty for what we want is a good idea.

However, you may want to be prepared for being overwhelmed with His answer.

As I sit here I realize I've forgotten the sound of the ocean created by the air handlers on the building next door; it is a sudden comfort to me. It's early (for me) on a Monday morning and I've dishes and laundry to put away, floors to Hoover, grades to enter into the grade book, a cable box to ready to return, and taking a shower and getting dressed to go to university this afternoon would be a really good thing.

Surveying my life I realize that the bills are okay, I've some money in my pocket, gas in the car, food in the pantry, cat food on the shelf, cigarettes, and the hope of a new client coming on board this week to get me finally on firm ground.

But, there is more to my life than that – much, much more. There's my position at the university, a second position which will make my car payment to start in October, there's my Judaism classes on Tuesday night, and my CoDa meeting on Wednesday; and ... well ... there's Jacob; the cherry on top of the sundae.

I was in a very good place Friday evening when Jacob sent me a thank you note for having sent him a card marking our six month anniversary; I answered it quickly with a short note saying it was true and left for Temple. But, I didn't make it to Temple on time. As I passed the gas station, I was reminded to get gas; so I turned around and filled the tank. In doing so, I realized I had forgotten my cell phone. Soooo, turned around and went back home to get it as I had this really sick feeling in my stomach that I needed to.

I don't know why I even checked my emails; but, I did, and Jacob had sent yet another note, to which I responded and left. After Temple I went and got some cigarettes and cat food; then home.

I puttered around the house, not really wanting to vacuum, but, needing to finish up my homework postings and entering attendance for the day. There was not much to do and all night to do it. By eight o'clock Jacob and I started with the e-mails again; nice ones, short ones; each trying to figure out what to do. Then, something changed. About ten o'clock, I was being a smart aleck and asked him if he wanted to come over for the night; he responded, "No! Actually I want you to come here and possibly stay the weekend!"

It was the first time he'd ever made such a concrete invitation; I read the words about ten times before I answered, "Do you mean this as I can be there within the hour."

I was afraid. I was afraid he'd say no; I was afraid he'd say yes; I was afraid that all the problems we'd had before we'd have again; and I was afraid that I had no idea what I was going to do to stop them.

Even though I knew it was late, I still called my CoDA sponsor. I told her what was going on, I told her I didn't know what to do; we talked for quite some time as Jacob and I was trading e-mails. Several messages came through loud and clear:

1. Don't react to anything he says; stop, think, then act.
2. Don't seek perfection, seek progress.
3. If what you've done in the past isn't working, then don't do it.
4. Try to end everything on a good note.

By the time we'd finished talking, I was packed for the weekend, and awaited Jacob's call. It didn't take long before he called and we were agreeing we'd been through some real hard times, we had something good, as he put it, "I need to take your stuff; you need to take mine, and we need to work through it" and yes, I could come for the weekend.

Armed with my plan of action, I was as giddy as a school girl, on my drive over. He carried my stuff in the house and helped me get settled; then, well, he did something strange – he turned on the music. And until nearly dawn, we sang off key, (well, at least I did!), we laughed, we danced, we talked, we enjoyed each other's company, and he told me he loved me at the same time I was thinking that I loved him.

Yet, we were both afraid of the morning after, when everything would change. We realized the cycle of his wall coming up, and me reacting to it; he said he'd try not to put the wall up and I said I'd try not to react to it if he did. And it worked!

Saturday was a time filled with just enjoyment of each other, light conversations, little things that showed we were making progress in the right direction. And Sunday? Well, it just doesn't get any better than talking for five straight hours about all the tough stuff;

working out all the boundaries; realizing that we are each different in the way we think and the way we move from one level to the next; and figuring out what the other needs and if/how we can meet them.

It wasn't just up to me anymore to make concessions; to make changes; it was up to him as well. For the first time, he was initiating the changes he felt he needed to make, he was willing to make; and I did the same thing.

Two years ago January I asked the Almighty to send me someone to love, who would love me; who I would be good for, and who would be good for me; and some one who we would be good for G-d. I just wasn't prepared when He exceed my wildest expectations.

TO BELIEVE

"You are not a good writer.

You are a GREAT writer."

As he talked, I could tell, his words were true. The truth showed in the twinkle in his eyes, the lilt to his voice, the excitement he portrayed, and the glow in his face. He believed his words; he believed in my talent ... he believed in ... me.

He didn't just sit there and tell me all the things he liked about my work; oh, no, he went one step further and started telling me all the avenues he thought I should explore to fully utilize my talents.

He was one of a small group who shared his beliefs. And sometimes, just sometimes, the difference between success and failure is having just one other person in the world who believes in us.

I have that now and I couldn't be more ... complete for it.

SANCTUARY

Here I sit once again at the keyboard.

This time, however, I have nothing to write.

So, why is this a comfort to me? I've spent the better part of the last year, writing essays, expressing myself, looking at the world through the glasses of my life's experience; yet, somehow sitting here on the front patio, again sporting Jacob's white terry bathrobe, as he sleeps soundly, I find myself with nothing to say.

There are no issues to be resolved; no problems to solve; no hassles to work out; so, um, what do we do now?

We had gone from off-again to on-again with the trading of a half-dozen e-mails and a simple phone call. Both of us "knew" we didn't want to throw away the good stuff just because of the bad; yet, we didn't know how to separate them – keep the good, work on the bad, and stay the hell away from the ugly!

Our lives are in a really good place right now; his business is growing nicely; I just picked up a second job not JUST to make the car payment, but to also get what I need for my Mustard Seed Project; and we're both ... well ... content; as if we are resting in our own self-made sanctuary. It's not just me who's been doing the changing this time – it's him; I could hear it in his voice this week, I could feel it in the hug he gave me this morning; and I could see it in the way he got into the music last night.

No, we're not perfect – but for right this minute we are perfect for each other. I'm not going to say we won't slide back into old habits, but I will say we are learning how to deal with the other's bad habits and make each other ... better.

I'd like to think the Almighty is smiling at this latest turn of events; resting for all the hard work He put into us; and confident that win, lose, or draw, we are doing what He planned for us all along.

BROKEN

I am broken.

And I've no idea how to fix it.

For all the hoopla I've given about being good alone, for being better with the right person and not so good with the wrong one; I've been lying to myself.

The fact is, I found the right person in Jacob; he just didn't want me; not right now, not in the foreseeable future; not in any type of real relationship. For as good as we were together; for as compete a union as I've ever seen; I've been played a fool.

I believed in him, in us; in the fairy tale that good does win over evil; that if you work hard and do your best good things will come; that true love does survive.

Like I said, I've been a fool. Why? Because, I forgot a few things in the mix. I forgot that it doesn't matter how good I see it if the other person doesn't see it, value it, or want it. I forgot that I am not in control, of this relationship or anything else in my life; the Almighty is. And I forgot that sometimes, just sometimes, the pain of loving someone does not overcome the joy.

I'm learning those lessons now.

So what do I do? I hurt, and I cry, and I long – but – I still go on with the matters of my life; I go to university; I work; I struggle to pay my bills; I go to Judaism classes; I go to my CoDA meetings; I partake in the celebration of the High Holy Days.

And I fake it – boy do I fake it.

I pretend to enjoy the events of my life as they are unfolding; I am truly grateful, but the hope – well – the hope is gone; it was the part that was broken. I don't know how to have the hope; to recapture the dream of what we had; to trust the silence as it has again betrayed me.

Yet, I don't KNOW that Jacob has walked away; I don't KNOW that we are over; I don't KNOW that what we had will never be again. I just FEEL that it has. And maybe this is where the hope lies; that maybe when I've got all my other stuff in order, we can try again – I can make clear to him what my needs are and he will NOT run away.

Right. Who am I kidding? If he has been running away from me since the beginning, what makes me think things are going to change? Hope. Ahhh, the hope that I've not wasted all of this for nothing; that the good I see was really there; that we didn't screw up the gift G-d has given us; and that with time, we will be again.

And if I can fake this long enough, maybe the pain will go away; maybe again I can be whole; maybe again … I can be all that G-d has in store for me.

Therein lies the hope.

OVER

When do you know it's over?

Or don't you?

Sometimes it's really cut and dried; one person screams, "IT'S OVER!", slams the door on their way out; and you never hear from them again.

Sometimes it's not – the phone calls dwindle, the meetings either get shorter or further apart or the excuses as to why you can't met start coming.

Sometimes one person SAYS it's over, but then keeps coming back, confusing the situation with alcohol or drugs or dependency issues. Sometimes there is a rough patch where one says, "Please, don't give up on me," then within the week, makes it very clear that they don't want to be with you for any other reason than a business deal.

At what point do you have to ask yourself, "Do I continue to fish or cut bait?" When does the hope of things being better become overridden by the patience you need to exhibit to make it that way; and, what if it doesn't? What if in the dance of taking one step forward and two steps back, you realize you are dancing ... alone?

What if in the process of waiting, all you are doing is postponing the inevitable? So, what do you do?

First you realize that just because they SAY they don't want a relationship, doesn't mean it's true.

Second, you realize that they will either come to recognize that what you have to offer is what they want; or if they don't, YOU don't want them anyway.

Third, this is the tough part, you realize that your emotions are controlled by your own thoughts; so, you take the good and relish them, you let the bad ones slide; BUT you have faith that the Boss not only knows what he is doing, but he has your back.

That's a lot to do, but it answers the question, "Do I continue to fish or cut bait?" with the answer; you enjoy sitting on the bank, watching the river go by, take comfort in the warm sunshine; appreciate the beauty around you – and IF a fish happens to hit your line, well, then that's just a bonus.

SO ... NOW WHAT?

My Dearest Jacob.

It's me again.

Nice job on the curve ball, Dude! I cannot believe I swung at the dirt on that one!! Sheesh! Even more so, I can't believe that you could knock me off my feet that quick. Then again, you do touch my heart so very easily, dear.

Sorry about my little freak out there – won't go down that road again!! Anyway, got my bearings back and the reason I'm writing is just to let you know I'm looking at going out of town for a bit and, well, didn't want you to worry.

It's really not all about me as I really hope you're okay and whatever the situation is has either fixed itself or you've got a new perspective on it.

Take care love; hope to hear from you soon.

Bye for now.
C

~~

But, it didn't fix itself, it just got worse.

SUMMARY

Did you see a parallel to an issue in your own life? The following ten questions may help you gain new perspective on how to manage it.

Questions to ponder:

1. Is this issue bigger than me?

2. What is my part in resolving the issue?

3. Is now the right time?

4. What's stopping me?

5. How do I remove the barriers?

6. What resources will I need to get started?

7. What resources do I have?

Answers to Act on:

8. What isn't working?

9. What is working?

10. What's the next step?

To do List:

Step 1

March

Step 2

Came to believe that a Power greater than ourselves could restore us to sanity.

~ *Alcoholics Anonymous*

CLEAN HOUSE

My Dearest Jacob,

The snow is falling, I've decided not to go out of town; so, I'm sitting here with nothing to do and all kinds of time to do it in. I wish I were spending the time with you.

But, as I can't, my thoughts turn to you ... to the words we've traded ... to the meaning behind them ... to the feelings that you've awaken in me ... to the time we've spent together ... and now, well, the silence.

It is the silence more than anything that confuses me. Although I realize there is nothing I can do ... I'm not used to feeling helpless, to being shut out, maybe this is a good thing? I don't know. I'm just trying to figure this out and I can't cuz you won't talk to me. I don't know why you shut me out; what happened to encourage the silence; if this is temporary or permanent; or if this is just the way you get when you get scared, confused, angry, or something else and it will pass. Maybe this is a good thing to find out now.

I have faith that if G-d wants us to be together nothing I do will stop it; and if He doesn't, nothing I do will make it happen. I just wish I knew what He wanted. I thought He made us come together -- I'm guessing I was wrong.

All I do know is that I'm rambling -- looking stupid -- am afraid of losing the best thing that's ever walked into my life -- missing you terribly -- hurting for reasons I don't even understand ... and there's not one thing I can do about it. I hope to hear from you again; I need you in my life; I am hands down better with you than I am with myself. I think you are as well.

If you ever wonder why I'm always talking with the "I" in the sentence it's because I'm showing you my thoughts -- I can't speak for you, nor think for you. I'm trying to lay my cards on the table and say -- this is as I see it; it's then your turn to show me what your take is on it and then WE can come up with what WE think.

One of the things I've done in the last three days is to become "clean" too. I've purged myself and my things of every other man I've ever known, but my sons. There is no more blender man; not that he hasn't tried, mind you, but that each time he does something YOU come into my mind and I am NOT going to jeopardize what we have for that SOS (Sack of Shit.) I've made it very clear to others who've made an attempt I am "off the market". It's easy for me to do this cuz you've wiped them all away for me and I've nothing to give them and everything I need is ... well ... you.

I'm ready, love, if you want me.

With grace,
C

THE MORNING AFTER

Every relationship has a period of time where if there are going to be problems, this is the time for them.

Ours was the morning after.

I thought about this time period as I was in it with Jacob; one more time I found myself waking up in his bedroom a month after he woke up in mine; one more time I found comfort in being in a place that made me feel at home; one more time with the realization that every aspect of my life that had been an issue with another was not an issue now. I started the coffee and made my way to the back deck and then lit my first cigarette of the day.

There it sat, in the corner; ready for me to use. The surprise was not in there BEING a beer can cum ashtray, but that I knew him so well that I knew there WOULD be one.

Knew him so well; odd term that. There was much I knew about him; the curve of his back, the joy in his eyes, the way he liked his coffee or kept his home, the way his touch would comfort me; and the way his standard answer for anything he wasn't sure of was, "*Really*?" with a sudden lilt to his voice. I knew many of his secrets, his fears, the things that made him laugh or worry; the things that drove him crazy, the love and respect he had for his family; the hardships he was trying to overcome; and where his strengths and weaknesses lay. What I didn't know was how to overcome "the morning after" that always seemed to be the undoing of us.

Our pattern was one of simplicity; we'd get together, have a great time, get to a great place; move our relationship one step forward; and then the morning after would hit. His wall would come up, I'd get really nervous because I could feel it; then the fear on both our parts would escalate the situation from really good to really bad. We'd bring out the absolute worse in each other; we'd go our separate ways; time would pass ... and we'd start all over again.

My hope was, maybe *this* morning we could figure it out.

As I waited for the coffee to perk, I went into his office and got some paper from the printer, and wished I'd brought my laptop. I went back to the deck and started to write, enjoying the sunshine and comfort of being in his home in one simple act. I recalled all the really good stuff we'd said to each other the night before; all the issues we'd cleared the air about; all the progress I could see in our just standing still mode.

Then again, he wasn't up yet; the problem time had not arrived; the time when I felt his wall would come up and I'd be left again on the outside.

I went to get my coffee and that was when he joined me in the kitchen. I poured us each a cup and listened to him ramble about bits of nothing to break the silence. That was different. We walked to the back deck, still him talking and me being quiet. I went back to my paper and he stood next to me. A few moments passed and he moved away; still rambling. When I got to the end of the sheet, I found myself at a good stopping point.

I put pen and paper to the side and went to sit next to him. When I asked at one point what he wanted me to do – he said, just listen. So, I did. One thing lead to another and he actually let me help him. Again, something new. Again, the hope was there that maybe this time we'd work out this stumbling block. But, he started to back away from me – I'd take a step forward; he'd take a step back. So, I stood still and he calmed down.

I left happy; he was happy. I'd done my best to stay within the confines he'd set for us. Needless to say that it was a surprise when he called me and I'd not yet made it home. He said he called just to say thank you. It was nice, but then, old habits came into play and as we'd decided he'd call me later in the afternoon, I asked to confirm this.

He started with the old issue of me trying to push this too hard, me not relaxing, me not being grateful for what we had but being greedy for what we didn't ... me ... me ... me.

Two steps forward, one step back.

I went about the rest of my day; and was rushing around to get ready for evening services when he called. I was ever so pleased that he did; however, I had to cut the conversation short with assurances I'd call him back in just a few minutes.

When I did – I got the machine; so I left a message saying I'd be free after seven and to please call me.

He didn't.

I sent him an e-mail later in the evening saying how proud I was of his taking advantage of an opportunity that was presented to him. What I didn't say was how much I really wanted to be with him and realized I wasn't invited.

He didn't respond.

The next evening I sent him an email saying that I hoped he was having a great day and told him some of the things that was happening in my life.

I added another with just a PS stating if he wanted company, I was free.

It was answered with an excuse of why he couldn't/wouldn't/didn't want to see me. The exchange continued; but briefly.

We are now back where we started from.

For all the good that we see in each other; for all the wonderful stuff that we share; there is still a wall around him that I can't get through as I'm not invited; there is still a hollow feel to it all that engulfs me with sadness.

They say some things just need time; that things will work out in G-d's time, not our own time; to let go and let G-d. I'm one to believe that things don't just need time, they need progress. And when there is no forward movement, and there is no standing still, there is a sliding backwards; and that is when you let go … for good.

What scares me the most is something that we disagree upon. Where I am one to believe that if G-d wants something to happen, there is nothing I can do to mess it up; and if He doesn't want it to happen there is nothing I can do to make it happen. Jacob is one to believe that if it was meant to happen that we CAN mess it up and lose it. My fear is that he is right, and he's doing everything in his power to prove it.

IS CHEATING A STATE OF MIND?

When is a relationship exclusive?

Perhaps when talking to another feels like … cheating.

I'd known him for some time; we'd chatted, had dinner, had a good first kiss, and talked sexy on the internet. But then tax season hit; and as he's a tax accountant, his life was thrown into the toilet. The last thing I remember about our relationship was me saying, "Get back to me after March."

And he did.

Today.

He was under the impression, as I'd given him no reason to believe otherwise, that I wasn't seeing anyone seriously. And I wasn't, was I?

I could see where our conversation was heading, so I punked out and said I had a meeting to attend; yeah, right; a meeting with my own mind perhaps, but not with another human being.

I needed some time to think; to sort out my emotions; to figure out where my boundaries now lay.

It wasn't just that after three months of nothing he unexpectedly contacted me TODAY; it was more like he was the THIRD guy from my past who chose TODAY as their day of re-entering my life. Why? What was so very special about TODAY?

And more importantly, sigh, what was I to do about it?

The first one was the cheater. That was a no-brainer; blow him off and go on.

The second one wasn't so easy; he was the second man who told me he needed some time to get his life together and he'd call me when he did. Well, apparently he got his act together and was ready for me to come back into his life.

Um, no, I don't think so. If a man thinks he can leave me hanging for six months and be surprised I wouldn't want to get back with him; he's just not the right guy for me.

The right guy. Hmm. This brings me to Jacob. We'd said a lot of things on Saturday night; things about him showing me I was important to him; drawing a line in the sand and starting it over right; me being patient and him being bold.

Yes, we said a lot of things, and it is my habit to hold others accountable for their words. Could I do anything less than to hold myself accountable for my words?

Did I mean it when I said I loved him? When he asked me if I was sure; and I said yes again? Was there no truth in my words when he asked me if I was his, and I said yes? Does it mean nothing when I give a man my words, yet, my actions don't honor them? Am I no better than all of the men I believed whose words turned to lies because their actions did not follow?

When I last saw Jacob on Sunday afternoon, his parting words were, "I'll call you later; probably even later today."

Well, in keeping with my silent promise to myself to let him take the lead in our relationship and WAIT for him to contact me, I DIDN'T send him an e-mail on Sunday; nor on Monday. It was one of the most difficult things I've had to do in a long time as every fiber in my being was screaming to contact him somehow. I went to bed last night concerned as I hadn't heard from him.

I knew it was sweeter if he came to me; I knew he took longer to make decisions than I did; and I trusted if I waited he would come to me. Saturday showed me how he took more time to do something than I do; and I realized this is a lesson I need to learn – how to be patient.

So, I closed my eyes last night, laying as he'd held me the last time he was here; I could smell his skin, his hair conditioner, his fabric softener, and his scent on my sheets and on his pillow.

I slept soundly only to wake up with the alarm wondering WHY he wasn't here; after all, I could smell him all around me. I was slightly saddened to find him no where to be found.

My concerns were laid to rest when I checked my e-mail this morning. Silently it sat there, an e-mail he sent me after I'd gone to bed. It was simple. The subject line said: Dinner. The message was: Hey! What do you think about coming over for dinner?

I was soaring!! I called my best guy buddy to tell him; and to ask for his advice on how to reply. It was as simple as the message: Good morning. I would like that very much. When? Would you like me to bring something?

I've waited all day for his response.

My hormones are raging; Jacob's little message had tripped my passions as he never failed to do; seemingly without trying.

I've been tempted three times today. Twice I cut them off at the pass. I felt like I was down to the wire with number three.

Do I continue waiting until Jacob decides to answer my simple question? But, the bigger issue is, do I trade gaining instant gratification for waiting for something that has all the markings of something really good; really long lasting?

If I am a woman of my word, I have two choices. 1. Consider myself 'off market' as I told Jacob I was and wait as is expected of me. Or, 2. Call Jacob and tell him the truth; that I'm going to cut it off with him to take a chance on something/someone else.

BAM!! There's the big, solid oak two-by-four between the eyes.

For a moment I thought my heart was going to stop beating. Seriously. My hormones had been raging all day driving my blood pressure up to 141/98; with a pulse of 107. The thought of making that phone call stunned me.

How could I do that? How could I call him after all I had said to him just three days ago and tell him it was over? It was in that moment I realized as difficult as waiting is, it didn't even come close to the near panic I felt at having to make that phone call. So, I did the only thing I could think of to do.

I wrote the third guy of the day an e-mail that simply said: Hey, you! It was nice to hear from you again. However, I think it only fair to tell you that I'm seriously seeing someone, so, I'm off market. I'll let you know if that changes.

Whew! It was a relief. I hadn't gone over that line – it was just IM – no phone calls, no promises I couldn't keep, and no meetings.

But, it still felt like cheating; and that's how I knew what I had with Jacob was real. I'd never felt like I was cheating before; I didn't like it now. However, it sure made waiting a whole lot easier. And I figured out what was so special about today; it was two months ago today that Jacob and I started talking; and the very first day that I realized what we have is real … even if only for me. Because Jacob didn't call … we didn't have dinner … it was nearly a week later when …

BLANK SLATE

I faced another blank page; another morning after.

This time, I'd sneaked a peak at the Playbill

I sat in bed last night, "catching up" on my daily devotionals regarding my co-dependent tendencies.

The book I was reading talked about anger issues, letting go, trust issues, and well, how to just enjoy today; how to let being good and being good enough RIGHT NOW be enough.

However, being the over-achiever I am I sneaked a peak at today's message, and well, the first line read: STOP TRYING TO MAKE IT HAPPEN.

Did the Almighty know?? Did He know I'd pick up that book last week? Did He know hat I needed to hear that message last night? That Jacob would be calling me at 3:18 in the morning asking me to please come over? Or, and here's a big one – that once again I would be facing yet another morning after?

The morning after was an odd time for us; a time where everything said or done the night before may or may not be discounted, may or may not hold true, may or may not be built upon this morning, or may or may not be ... real. For the difference between the night before and the morning after was determined by just how much Jacob had had to drink; just how very much he remembered, and of course, just how much he had done to get what he wanted.

Although when he called he'd say just how much sex he was after, more times than not, there was no or little sex when I arrived. It wasn't that he didn't want it, it was just that he wanted MORE than just to get laid. That is what his actions told me; that is what I wanted to believe; and that is what just talking, or laughing, or singing, and not having sex proved to me.

When in passing yesterday my thoughts turned to the "next time" with Jacob I thought I'd hit upon the perfect solution to "the morning after"; I'd just leave before he got up.

In my over think mode I ran through the possible scenario's from him getting up before I left, to him calling before I got home, to him just not bothering to call again. Of course all of those actions equated to an elephant crapping in the middle of the living room floor that no-one wanted to talk about. Every one sees the elephant; sees the mess, smells the mess; knows someone's going to have to clean up the mess; but no one wants to do it. Least of all, me.

STOP TRYING TO MAKE IT HAPPEN. Sigh.

As I sit on the back deck, under the shade of the patio table umbrella writing this (3:30 am is NOT the time to try to pack my laptop), I catch a glimpse of my reflection in the patio doors. I'm curled up in a high patio chair, sporting his big white terry cloth bathrobe (didn't have time to pack jammies) and my NY Yankees baseball cap (forgot the hair ties too!) sipping his favorite chocolate flavored coffee, and using a beer can as an ashtray. I notice something else as well.

There is a smile that I just can't seem to wipe off my face; it completes the look of contentment very well.

Yes. I could leave right now before he got up; but the question is: why would I want to? Of course the obvious answer is to avoid the elephant in the living room. Avoid – for today that is – cuz the elephant isn't going to go away by being ignored. Fact is, the longer I ignore it, the bigger the mess is going to get.

So if I'm not going to leave before he gets up; the only other option is to stay. And do what?

STOP TRYING TO MAKE IT HAPPEN. I didn't read enough to figure out how to do this, but I can hazard a guess; just stop, enjoy the right now, and let tomorrow take care of itself.

It's not a bad place to be in, fact is, it's pretty darn comfortable – for now.

LISTENING TO THE ALMIGHTY

"I thought you were too screwed up to love anyone.

I was wrong. You just can't love me."

The words escaped my mouth and echoed in my head before I even had time to think about them. I hung up the phone and didn't answer it when it rang again as I knew it would.

I was tired; more than tired of trying to convince Jacob I was worthy of him, that I was good for him, and hearing of all the reasons why he couldn't love me. That the only time we were really good was when he was too drunk to let his fear overshadow everything else. When he was sober; he was afraid. When he'd been drinking all was right with the world.

I was tired of the e-mails, the text messages, the late night phone calls which normally started off with him telling me how wonderful I was, which escalated to the various reasons of why I wasn't for him, and ended with him asking if he could come over.

Why in the world would I want to invite someone over who made it very clear they couldn't/wouldn't/didn't love me? Was I so lonely for human companionship I would settle for this? Was I so (forgive me for this one) horny I'd take any man to my bed? Was the lady acting like a whore for no other reason than to feel the touch of another?

No, she wasn't. I wiped away the new found tears from my face and admitted what I was doing was hanging on to people who no longer wanted me; and the "why" was no longer important. It was with suddenly clarity through the late night hour I realized not letting go was in essence telling the Almighty He didn't know what He was doing; that I really did know what was better for me than He did.

But, I didn't. I'd listened only half-heartedly to His attempts to tell me to find myself, get myself out of the gutter, get up where I belonged; do that which made me happy, not just paid the bills; but I didn't really believe Him.

I've been told you can't find Mr. Right with Mr. Wrong standing in the way. Wasn't this happening to me now? Wasn't Jacob just another Mr. Wrong who I thought was Mr. Right standing in the way; showing me only part of what was really available to me; leading me down a path that at first looked like the yellow-brick road, but ended up nothing more than a trail of broken glass.

I thought I should feel angry, sad, frustrated; but I didn't. I was … thankful; grateful even for seeing bits and pieces of the type of man I wanted in my life; the type of life I wanted to live; and how I wanted to live it.

Through His design I was given the opportunity to find some direction in my life; all of my life from my work, to my studies, to my family and yes, to the men in my life.

The phone rang again and I did the only thing I could think of; I shut the phone off. I rolled over in bed, whispered a "Thank You" to the Almighty, and then added, "I am listening."

BOUNDARIES

"Stop being such a spoiled brat!" I yelled.

Unfortunately, I was yelling at myself.

Many times I have asked, and rarely has it been answered, but, when is enough, enough, and when is wanting more, just plain greed? Perhaps for answer, I can turn to my grandchildren.

As the three of them had come to stay for a week (for the first time without parents) I found myself in schedule overload between meals, and caretaking, and things to do; and they were rolling with the punches. A typical day began to settle into a pattern: get up, get breakfast, get dressed. Then clean up the house, take naps, eat lunch, go to the science center or the zoo or the park or where ever; come home, eat dinner, go to the pool, then ready for and get them to bed. By the end of the day, I was exhausted, but, I still had studies and friends to catch up with.

It was the trip to the zoo that brought my question into full light. My only grandson is a real treasure; he's big, and helpful, and kind. But, he IS eight-years old and as such has the patience, energy, and attention span of an eight-year-old. I knew I was facing a temporary cash flow problem, so wanted to watch what we spent at the zoo. I really HATE not being in a financial position to give those around me everything they want; but, then again I realize, that if I did, where would it end?

I ramble.

So it was at the zoo I realized that a pattern was forming; he wanted to ride the train; it was five dollars per person; I cheated a bit and told them both girls were under two; so the trip only cost ten dollars. A side benefit was that I didn't have to push, carry, or walk the distance around the zoo.

The first stop brought us to the bird house. The oldest granddaughter wanted to see it. We went – it was cool (in both temperature and sights to see). The youngest granddaughter got the surprise of her little life when she realized that the blue tile was safe to walk on and not the water it looked like. My grandson wanted to go to the gift shop. This I said no to; but I did say yes to going to see the big cats.

The second stop brought us to the penguin house which both kids wanted to see; again I said no to the gift shop – but the question of the carousel came up. We got something to eat, and as we sat there, my grandson started in on wanting to ride the carousel; he was relentless. This was not JUST a matter of money now – this was something else indeed. There are few people who know this about me, but the carousel makes me sick – I mean, turn green, get dizzy, and throw up SICK.

So, we were at a crossroad; do I give them what they want (the carousel ride), at the expense of the money and the chance of me being ill; or do I say no and face disappointing them. I gave in and we went. And I got sick – but – not as much as I normally would. However, it suddenly didn't matter as it was now on to the next thing.

I spent the rest of the afternoon thinking about this cause and effect, this need and fulfillment, situation and I got to wondering ... am I doing the same thing?

With my on-again, off-again relationship with Jacob I find we are in the off-again position. I let my needs be known (kindly, gently) and he got scared and ran away ... again.

When I couldn't fulfill the endless needs of my grandchildren, I felt inadequate; could he see my needs the same way and he too feel the inadequacy? Perhaps he did. Maybe my requests that he saw as frightening, were actually just the normal progression of a relationship; and as such, he felt that if he fulfilled them it would mean we were IN a relationship. Is that such a bad place to be? Maybe it is ... right now.

Though I saw my needs as meeting the basic requirements of a standard relationship; he did too ... and that's what scared him. He didn't want a relationship, he made that very clear; but, he did want all the benefits of one under a different name ... friendship.

There are boundaries for friendships and boundaries for relationships; knowing what they are and following them determines which is which. Giving them different names doesn't change what they are, it doesn't change the emotions felt; it just changes the expectations and the liberties.

I realize that my friends do take certain liberties; they know they are a priority on my list; that I will always have their back, and I will always give them the straight skinny as I see it. I am there to help them, and they are here to help me, without question or judgment or fear.

My friends, however, DON'T call me at three am, they don't ask me to come and see them, they don't sleep with me; those freedoms are reserved for the man in which I am having a relationship. In this case, those are freedoms and liberties I freely gave to Jacob. And in return, I expected a certain level of respect, of appreciation, of consideration – no different from what I would expect from my friends, just on a higher level.

I realize now, that although he wanted my commitment of being in a relationship, he couldn't give what he asked for. Although he wanted all the benefits of being in a relationship, he used it under the guise of friendship. He set the boundaries for a friendship, yet, used the boundaries of a relationship to do so.

As we rode the train to the last stop I realized that he called a tiger a lion and didn't think I could tell the difference; or maybe he couldn't tell the difference for his fear. Either way, I have hope in one little phrase: right now. Although I am one to believe change takes effort, it also takes time; and he needs the time to catch up to recognize the boundaries and their differences; or stay in the dark with someone else.

SUBSTITUTES

He wasn't a *bad* man.

He just wasn't the *right* man.

As I watch the sun, just barely up as it is, giving all about me the grey-light of early morning, I smile. It's a smile that has been ever so long in coming back to me. But, wait, I'm giving away the ending. ☺

There was a point last night when I was sitting on the parlor bed, surrounded by files and students' papers, halfway listening to the Yankees/Indians game, dressed in my favorite jeans and cotton camisole, when I looked up and realized – Life is good! (Okay, fine, so the Yankees got spanked, that's not the point! Lol)

As today is Friday I had made it through my week of anniversaries of "terrors", had made one rent payment on Monday, was going to make another this morning – still wasn't sure how the car payments were going to be made – but was happy that the utilities were on and many were not due again until month's end. I had a bit of extra money that I could use to either get my car fixed or go spend my long weekend with my son and his family, I chose the latter and would be leaving right after university class this afternoon, and although I had withdrawn from my university degree class (to start it again at month's end) I still had the upcoming Hebrew class to look forward to starting and an interview for a life-coaching position next week.

There was a long-lost feeling of contentment washing over me as I suddenly realized that I was right where I belonged, doing exactly what I was supposed to be doing, and the Almighty was smiling.

So, why is it, do you think, that last night, after I took a break from my work, grabbed a quick nap, then awoke and finished my work, I invited Biker Man over for some company of the "adult variety"? I don't know why – but I do know that it was the beginning of the strangest night I've had in a very long time.

There is no doubt in my mind that I missed Jacob to the nth degree; I missed his touch, the way he loved me, the way I felt safe in his arms, the way he recharged my batteries with a smile, a kiss, or a hug, the way his laugh would light up his eyes, the list was long. Not quite believing, but willing to test the theory, that any body really is better than no body; I figured it wouldn't hurt to partake in the activity with Biker Man. After all, I rationalized, Jacob had thrown me away; he'd made it clear we were no longer a couple. But, I forgot HE isn't the Almighty either!

So it was, as we lay on the sofa bed, one thing led to the natural path of another until I found myself gazing at the living room ceiling as Biker Man was doing what he thought would bring me pleasure and I was thinking to myself, "You know, this really isn't working for me." As if in reaction to my thoughts, he lost the spark, as that which was willing, was no more. I thought it odd this would happen at this moment; and was wondering if I could make it happen again, when I heard the Almighty say, "You can bet it isn't *going* to happen either."

"Why is that?" I asked Him.

I pictured the Almighty standing there with his arms folded across his chest, tapping his foot, giving me the "I don't bloody well think so look", and taking on that too-in-touch-with-his-feminine-side nasal tone. "Because I worked too hard and too long on the two of you for you to throw it away like this when all you have to do is wait to get what you want."

One thing stopped leading to another, and I made mention to him that it was okay, that we could get some sleep and try again. He professed to not knowing WHY this was happening and in the darkness, I smiled. I DID know why, and the Almighty confirmed the why, by saying, "You promised yourself to Jacob; I'm going to make you stick to the promise. You said you were his girl; you said you would be his forever, and ever; now, be woman enough to live up to your word."

I gave him another smile and said I would. But, the man laying next to me was a sudden ... curiosity. First he lay in the spooning position, holding me -- touching me as I wanted another to; and I heard the Almighty ask if I wanted Him to show Jacob this. I said, "Please do, and tell him the smile I'm wearing is because I'm thinking it is him laying with me." We chuckled at that.

Then Biker Man slowly, body part by body part, moved away from me until there was only one small patch of skin connecting us; I moved so he wasn't touching me at all. When I heard his breathing denote he was asleep, I got up, sat on the floor, and lit the last of too many cigarettes of the day.

I realized there was a lot of things I wouldn't allow anyone else to do that I gave Jacob free-reign of; body parts they couldn't touch, acts of love making I wouldn't perform for them, and the mere fact that we weren't in MY bed was an added barrier. I finished my cigarette, went to the bathroom, then ... well ... went and got into MY bed. As I lay there I realized this was MY bed and the only one I would share it with was Jacob; and until such time as I COULD share it with him, well, I'd share it with no one. "That's right," the Almighty said.

"Ya think?" I said jokingly, smiling at the darkness. For some reason, I got the idea in my head that if the Almighty wanted Jacob and I to be together the man sleeping on my sofa bed in the living room and I wouldn't make love when I got up; and if the Almighty DIDN'T want Jacob and I to be together, we would. How this was going to work out was beyond me but I felt is was some kind of proving point.

I awoke several hours later in the same position I fell asleep in; which denoted that I slept like a rock for the first time in weeks. I rolled over and smiled; suddenly I realized it wasn't yet daylight, my alarm hadn't gone off – and – well, there was a naked man sleeping in the living room on my sofa bed!

Quietly I slipped into the bathroom and peeked out the door into the living room. Much to my relief – he was gone; sometime during the night, as I slept like a rock, he'd gotten up, gotten dressed, and ... left. My smile widened as I fixed myself a cup of coffee and while it was heating ... made my bed, made up the sofa bed, started the laundry of all the bedding that was on the sofa bed ... and ... well ... took a shower. I felt this overwhelming need to remove all traces of him from me and my things so I even sprayed all the areas he had touched with air freshener.

He was gone and in his place was a feeling of ... contentment. I started my day with a smile which I've not done in weeks; I'm writing which I haven't done in far too long; I hear the Almighty laughingly say, "See, I told you so!" and in doing so confirming that Jacob will be back and things will work out between us. How, and when, is still up to the Almighty.

I have ... hope ... that not only is life good but it's getting better and better every day. Once again, the Almighty has confirmed in my life that He IS the Almighty, not me, certainly not

Jacob, and definitely NOT the man who slept on my sofa bed! For some reason, I'm really good with that. ☺

STRATEGY

He moves here; I move there; the dance continues.

We either both win, or we fall on our asses.

"Ahhh," as Indigo in *The Princess Bride* would say, "I have no head for strategy; that's Fazinni's job." Well, I realize I have no head for strategy either; at least not while running on four hours of sleep and NO coffee. But, I do find myself in the same place as on other mornings when I've awoken at Jacob's house; facing the ever-dreaded morning after.

As I sit here in the early morning (well, at least for THIS morning!) sunlight, my cat playing somewhere in the front yard, the cicadas making their usual racket, the chimes bonging gently in the wind; I wonder, who is my Fazinni?

Passing the glass chess set he has arranged on the wet bar between his office and the living room, I casually make the standard opening move; king's pawn ahead two spaces. I go to move the other's pawn and realize that something is just not quite right. This move was to result in both pawns facing off; yet, on this board, the clear pawn would easily take the frosted one.

Hmm. That's not right, I thought to myself. The board was right; the pieces were all there; and the order was rook, knight, bishop, king, queen, bishop, knight, rook. I check the other side and the set up is exactly the same. Ahh, there's the rub! As any chess player will tell you, the set up can't be *exactly* the same from both directions for the Queen must always begin on her color; i.e. a clear queen on a clear square; a frosted queen on a frosted square. Smiling to myself for having figured this out, I switched the king/queen set up and made the opening move again. This time the face-off resulted and for the moment, all was right with my world.

But, I hadn't planned it that way; it happened by ... design? Hmm. If it is true that we need the really bad days to show us what the really good days are, then yesterday was the standard to judge all the good days.

Earlier in the week, I had turned my relationship with Jacob over to the Almighty, simply stating, "If you want it to work, it will; if you don't, there's nothing I can do to make it work." And I did nothing.

Well, in that area; in the other areas of my life I worked diligently; which led to all areas coming to a head by the end of the day yesterday. In one day, I had figured out the snafu in my student loan application so now my last class would be paid for; I had talked to my sponsoring Rabbi for my Judaism classes and found I didn't need to set up a payment plan as they had a scholarship; and, well, miracles of miracles – I had a job. It wasn't just A JOB; it was a GREAT JOB; and although I'm not counting my chickens before they are hatched, I am celebrating in the good news.

The only thing missing was sharing it with Jacob. I had thought about calling him that evening; but, I didn't. I figured, if I turned the relationship over to the Almighty, He REALLY didn't need me meddling in His affairs. ☺

So, although I normally go to bed at one o'clock, I convinced myself that it was a Friday night and I really could stay up later. By ten after one, Jacob called. I was sooo excited I could barely contain myself! I was, as they say, as giddy as a schoolgirl as I recounted for him all the happenings of the day.

Oddly enough, he listened to me; he laughed; he was happy. So, why the excuses when I asked him to come over? Hmm. I didn't know. That was his move; my counter move was to ask him to ask me to come over. He did. I did. And we stayed up until five a.m. just talking and enjoying the other's company.

Or maybe we were just … stalling. We didn't want to go to bed; because we didn't want to wake up and face yet another … morning after; another morning of him "not feeling well", of us not being able to talk because he couldn't think straight, or another morning of way too many beer cans in the trash compactor, . Sigh.

Right now, it's about 3:30 in the afternoon; I'm on the front porch writing; Jacob is watching golf on the tele; and we are … comfortable. Yeah, it's hot outside; so I'm sporting a pair of his cotton shorts – which with the top rolled down don't look too bad. I'm also enjoying my first cup of coffee for the day. I guess it would be different if after he got, we didn't go back to bed – a couple of times -- so when we actually got UP for the day it was one in the afternoon.

Yes, I did make the trip to the grocer for coffee (as he was out hence the reason for no coffee first thing in the day); and the gas station for smokes; and the fast food joint for food. I figured it was a fair trade as he bought them and I went and got them.

Something's different; he is calmer, more relaxed, and he is making some changes in just his ways. His best guy friend mentioned it as well yesterday; and I heard it in his call last night. He mentioned baby steps last night; he takes his and I take mine.

Always one for taking comfort in a plan, in a strategy, I'm finding that sometimes you don't need a plan; you just need to enjoy what you have. With all the happenings going on yesterday; all the miracles large and small; I'm finding today is a day of … rest. It is a day of truly enjoying that hint of a cool breeze which pops up in the hot August afternoon; a day of taking comfort in the silence; a day of no questions, no expectations, no demands. I'm realizing as well … the Almighty is my Fazinni. He does it so much better than I do. ☺

SUMMARY

Did you see a parallel to an issue in your own life? The following ten questions may help you gain new perspective on how to manage it.

Questions to ponder:

1. Is this issue bigger than me?

2. What is my part in resolving the issue?

3. Is now the right time?

4. What's stopping me?

5. How do I remove the barriers?

6. What resources will I need to get started?

7. What resources do I have?

Answers to Act on:

8. What isn't working?

9. What is working?

10. What's the next step?

To do List:

Step 2

April

Step 3

Made a decision to turn our will and our lives over to the care of God *as we understood Him.*

~ *Alcoholics Anonymous*

FEAR

There's something to be said for fear.

It can save a life; or destroy one.

In this case, it destroyed something wonderful; and there was nothing I could do to stop it. It's oftentimes been said of me that I am courageous, brave, and strong; that isn't true. What I am is incredibly selfish.

Now, selfish has had a bad rap over the years, and most think of selfish in the "spoiled brat" sense; some might argue I fit that description as well. Yet, there is another not so well known method of looking at the term, "devoted to or caring only for oneself" which colors my world.

When faced with a situation where my selfishness comes into play, I ask myself, "Am I so busy that I can't help a little old lady out of her car?" Of course not, so I take the two minutes out of my day and help her. "Am I so important that I can't put $5 in the box to help those less fortunate than I?" Of course not, so I put in $10. Or more importantly, "Am I the type of woman who will only accept a man on certain conditions?" No, so, I loved him unconditionally – and it scared the daylights out of him; so we both lost.

Fear is a strange duck. He believed that, "Fear comes when one of us feels the other has expectations that we can't meet." But, I believe it can come from our own expectations as well as other's expectations. Fear can come from inside as well as from outside; it can be sudden or a slow burn; it can be a reaction to what is happening or based on our thoughts of what might happen. Yet, regardless of all of those conditions, once realized it can be overcome.

It's not easy to live with fear; it's easier to face it – if you know how. As I see it, facing fear is making a decision. The question becomes, is it easier to live with this fear or to face it head on? Is it easier to be afraid that someone will realize all of our faults and that we are not the wonderful person they think we are; or to show them our faults one at a time and let them decide?

Ahh, therein lies the base of the situation. Whose decision is it? If we see our own faults, and we find them unacceptable, we believe others will do the same; hence, they will decide that we are unworthy.

The problem is what if they don't? What if what we feel are our weaknesses, they see as our strengths? What if what we see are our past wrongs and failings they see as that which made us stronger? And what if, just what if, we see all of who we are and compare it to who we think they are, and realize that we aren't good enough for them; and they think we are everything they'd hoped to find?

Whose decision is it?

If we take it upon ourselves to decide our worthiness for someone else we also take the risk of being wrong, and missing out on something that could just be everything we hoped beyond hope to find. If we allow others to decide for themselves, yes we do take the risk of not being as worthy as they think we are, BUT we also allow them the freedom to enjoy all the good that they see which is hidden or covered up in our view of ourselves.

There's an old saw, "Be careful what you wish for, you just might get it." I did; I just wish Jacob would have let me make my own decision instead of deciding for me. He was wrong.

FOLLOWING DIRECTIONS

Call Jacob.

No.

It wasn't the first time in my life that I had said no ... to the Almighty... just the most recent time. I didn't say no right away either; I preferenced it with a childish ranting that went something like this: WHY? So I can beg him to come back? So he can tell me how much he ISN'T in love with me? So he can fill my head with all his pretty words which turn to lies with his inaction? So he can lie to me, betray me, cheat on me ... AGAIN? No.

I was tired. I had worked very hard for three days and had two more days to go to get everything on my revolving to-do list done. Nine o'clock on a Saturday night is no time to address the subject of Jacob. The Almighty apparently thought otherwise. Yes, I missed Jacob terribly; I missed what we had; there was a void where he once lived in my heart, my mind, my soul. But, it didn't matter – he was the one who had walked away, destroyed at every turn all that we had, and had proven to me that he really had no use for me in his life. And here the Almighty was telling me to ... call him?

The odd thing was, between the time He told me to call him and the time my childish rantings begun, I had actually picked up the phone and was dialing Jacob's number. I hung up before the call went through. That is the way of my life; the Almighty tells me to do something, normally I do it without question. It works for me, generally.

About three o'clock in the morning, I awoke, with the Almighty's directive running through my head: Call him. This time I simply said "No" and rolled over and went back to sleep.

Sunday morning was yet another day filled with doing things ... for me. I had my shelves to paint, my bedroom curtains to sew, my weekly chores to do and a few extras to make the apartment look even nicer. I was content in the work I had done since Thursday: the touch-ups on my living room, my bathroom now the perfect shade of Fairy Lily Yellow, and the one wall in my office the same color. I'd graded all my papers, written a proposal for the VP, had finally cleaned my knives, had a head start on my own homework assignments, and had done two dozen other things that just made my life better. And each step of the way, I saw the Almighty's hand at work.

So, why was it on Sunday that everything I touched ... turned to mud? I had three little shelves to paint. It was a simple task compared to the monumental tasks I'd completed. The first shelf wouldn't take the paint; so I wiped it off. The second self looked HORRIBLE and by the time I got to the third shelf the paint fumes were making me sick. I chucked the whole mess out onto the patio and went to sew my curtains. It was a matter of taking curtains that were too long and making them into French Venetian curtains by simply sewing the folds I'd already pinned into them. I got about eight inches into the first one – and had to rip it out and start over; I got the first one done ... and had to rip out the second one. I stopped.

When things in my life are not going well, I refrain from chalking it up to a "bad day"; I stop, and talk to the Almighty, and change my course.

I poured a fresh cup of coffee, lit another of too many cigarettes, and sat at my desk. "Okay, Almighty," I said aloud. "What's the skinny?"

There wasn't an immediate answer, so I calmed myself from the frustrations, and asked again. Very quietly, He said, "I told you to do something, twice, last night and you said ... no."

He didn't need to say anything more. The tears streamed my face, the hurt filled my heart, but, I knew what I had to do. Jacob's voice on the answering machine ... calmed me somehow; touched my soul once again; and ripped out my heart knowing he wasn't mine. I left a trite message and went back to my coffee. Oddly enough, I was angry! Why would the Almighty want me to CALL him?? What purpose did it serve other than to hurt ME??

As I sat looking out at the sunny day, my thoughts swarmed ... the confusion, the anger, the hurt, the injustice of me giving myself to another just to be tossed away for no other reason than he could. And yet, the Almighty wanted me to CALL HIM. I didn't understand.

"Why," I whispered, "do you hurt me so? Why do you feel I need this pain?"

"Shh, my child," He said, "I didn't say TALK to him, I just said CALL him for it is not the pain of losing that you need, it is the moment of calm that his voice brings to you."

It wasn't worth it; but, getting my day back on track, doing all the other things I needed to do with the help of the Almighty ... was. It was a small price to pay for the rewards I received. It was also one more reassurance that when I follow the directions I'm given, the road isn't quite so bumpy. May I always remember the directions are for the path that I **need** to follow; not always the path I **want** to follow.

PLANS

They tell me pain is a great teacher.

So, when are my lessons over?

I hadn't planned on seeing Jacob Saturday before last. I hadn't planned on us getting back together and making some major steps in our relationship. I hadn't planned on stopping by Jacob's on the way to see my children on Friday. And I certainly hadn't planned on realizing when I did that he had been with another woman the night before either.

There was no way I could plan for the pain I am feeling now; the feelings of betrayal, of being tossed away, of losing all that I had invested in the relationship; and most of all, the feelings of foolishly trusting my emotions to one who had proven himself untrustworthy.

Now, what do I plan to do? Sigh. Cry. Hurt. Breathe. Go on. Do what I have to do to take care of me. Try not to think. Try not to … remember. Things are not going as … planned.

Or, maybe they are and I just don't know it.

When Jacob came back that Saturday, he filled my head with hollow dreams, filled my heart with empty promises, and he filled my soul with fake emotions; words turned into lies with inaction. I believed him; I accepted him; I forgave him without reservations.

And he betrayed me.

The real pain comes in knowing that I still love him; that I can see all the good stuff we could have had, if only he would have wanted it. But, he didn't want them or me; at every opportunity he told me so … with his inactions. I just didn't listen.

Now what? Where do I put all this pain? What do I do next? Where's the plan? I don't have one. I know what I have to do today to take care of myself; I know I need to go to work this afternoon; I know I need to work on my writing this morning; and sometime today I need to get the meds for my cat and start back up at school.

But, I don't feel like doing any of it. What I feel like doing is going back to bed, covering up my head, and sleeping for the next millennium. Of course this will do no one, including me, any good. It's still an option though.

Why is it, do you think, that we believe if another was in our life that our lives would be ... better? Why do we believe when another betrays us that it is somehow OUR fault? And to add to this ... why is it we believe when another has sex with someone else it is BETTER than the sex they had with us? Why do we believe these ... lies?

Who says if they were in our lives it would be better? If the pain they are causing us now is on a part-time basis, what makes us think if it were full-time that it would be better – not just more of the pain we are having now? Why do we think another's betrayal means we've done something wrong, something to cause it; or worse yet, we are some how NOT good enough so we forced them to someone else?

Why in the world would sex with someone new be better than sex that has taken several months to develop? It wouldn't. Fact is, the only thing sex with someone new is ... new. Yes, I will admit that sex with someone new has its appeal; however, there is little satisfaction in it; there is even less love to it; and above all – there is little to no commitment to it. No, I am NOT condoning his actions or justifying them in any way; what I am doing, however, is realizing that even though he slept with another, there is no way it could be better than him sleeping with me.

Unfortunately, for both of us, it was the straw that broke the camel's back.

Which brings me full circle to: what do I do now?

For all the justifications, for all the logic, for all the pain; the plain and simple truth is ... I have no idea. And maybe, just maybe, that *is* the plan. Do what I have to do today to take care of me – and let G-d do the rest.

I just hope my lessons are done soon; the pain is getting a bit difficult to stand. May I have faith that when things aren't working out the way I planned that they are working out exactly as G-d has planned.

ONLY

It's only been a week.

So why does it seem like so much longer?

A week ago today, right now, I was still asleep in Jacob's bed; I awoke to face five hours of soul searching, relationship building conversation; and left hearing his words, "I'll call you later."

Knowing him better than I had before, I thought he meant Tuesday or Wednesday; not my original time line of that afternoon. Yet, I can't help thinking it was an obligatory comment; he said it because he thought that's what I wanted to hear.

There's a lot of things I can't help thinking; first off, how I'm kidding myself into believing we have a relationship – though he used the word a dozen times last weekend and assured me on some level that we do; then there's the "I'm not good enough for him" which is a self-debasing measure; of course there is always the old I-gotta-DO-something train of thought which is a major relationship destroying measure; to the "Okay, Almighty, it's up to you" measure with the hope being the Almighty will see fit to make it work and maybe he'll call me; to finally end up at the "screw-it-I'm-outta-here" said to yourself goodbye measure.

I'm realizing a cycle here; one that I'm not sure how to break, one in which I see that something is missing, but I don't know what.

If you've read as many self-help/relationship books as I have (and I've read a plenty of them) they will tell you to let go, let G-d, and be good with it; how you can't control someone else, how you can ONLY do so much to further a relationship.

What they don't tell you, however, is how to feel good about yourself and the relationship when you're in this "down time", which is very similar to what Iyanla Vanzant has coined "The Meantime". She's written some wonderful works and has some very helpful takes on issues I've been dealing with in my life.

I know at this point I should be working on me, my issues, my life and life style; I know that I should detach myself from Jacob to the point where whatever he does or doesn't do has no effect on my life; I know that I need to find the joy of being alone and find value in just being; and that I should have faith that the Almighty not only knows what He's doing (as He does) but He has what's best for me at the fore front (which He also does).

Yes, I *know* all of that; I also *believe* all of it; however, if ONLY I could *feel* it, I'd be where I need to be. The chasm between what I know and what I feel is a kin to the Grand Canyon.

What I do is based on what I know. I clean my flat; I go to work; I look for opportunities that the Almighty sets before me; I concentrate on how to pay the bills; I give my time to my friends and making new ones; and I am good. Yet, there are these moments of ... disconnection ... moments when I've nothing to do and all kinds of time to do them where I just sit and breath and ... think. There are a great deal of joys happening in my life, with my studies, with my students, with the changes I'm going through; and they are ... diminished somehow as there is no one to share them with; no one to celebrate them with; and I am happy for the opportunity but saddened for the lack of sharing.

So, if I do what the books all say, and I let go, let G-d, and do become good with it; then what? See that's where the problem lies for me.

If I get to the point where I nether need nor want someone in my life; if I am totally good alone; then I will say goodbye to Jacob, and even more importantly, good bye to anyone else who comes along; I will get to the point where as I don't need/want anyone, I won't make the effort or put in the energy to even be bothered with another. I will become stronger, and more jaded, and a bit more confident, and I will lose something ... beautiful. I never want to get to that point; however, I can't keep going on the way I am pining for something that may or may not ever happen.

What frightens me is I'm almost to that point right now; and maybe, just maybe, that is the best place to be. To become the strong, confident person that I am; who needs nor wants no one; who can be enough just as she is; and even more importantly, who doesn't really care about anyone being in that position in her life.

Sigh.

The only way to do this, is to shut the door to my heart; to say good bye, walk away, and completely detach. Of course, there is always the chance that I won't 'attach' again, and I'm guessing that is a chance I'll just have to take.

I know it's better this way; to completely detach from another, to live my life dependent only on myself and the Almighty;

to get to the point where IF/WHEN Jacob calls, the answer is … no; as it will be for any other who tries to open that door. It will be a matter of living life in black and white and shades of grey; not the Technicolor version that it can be.

I'll be good with this, as I have no other choice; now, if ONLY I could feel it.

****

STOPPING

Another blank page; another morning after.

I was right back where I was before: STOP TRYING TO MAKE IT HAPPEN.

There is no doubt in anyone's mind, least of all mine, that what I was trying to make happen was for us to get to a comfortable place; a place where we could both just sit and breathe. And it had gotten to the point where me doing SOMETHING TO MAKE IT HAPPEN blew up in my face.

Jacob has a habit of talking in his sleep; unlike others, it's hard to tell that he's not awake when he does it. The only reason I know he IS still asleep is that his breathing rhythm doesn't change. So it was at this moment that his talking in the early morning hours came to the forefront.

We were both asleep, when he asked me, "You my girl?" I moaned an answer.

"Say the words," he whispered.

"Yes, baby," I replied.

"Forever?" he asked.

"Ummm, hmm," I replied.

"Say it," he whispered again.

"Yes, baby," I replied.

"Forever and ever?" he asked.

"Yes, baby, forever and ever," I said.

He pulled me closer and nuzzled into the crook of my neck, and whispered, "Please don't break my heart."

"I promise, I won't," I whispered back. I'm not sure how much time had passed when we had the very same conversation … again.

But in the morning light, it suddenly dawned on me that he too was trying to find this place; this place of trust and semi-commitment, the peace of mind that whispers "Yes, baby" as reassurance in the wee hours of the morning.

I didn't read enough to figure out how to stop trying to make it happen; but I can hazard a guess – again just stop. I'd like to believe it's the first step in opening the door and letting the elephant out of the living room.

SUMMARY

Did you see a parallel to an issue in your own life? The following ten questions may help you gain new perspective on how to manage it.

Questions to ponder:

1. Is this issue bigger than me?

2. What is my part in resolving the issue?

3. Is now the right time?

4. What's stopping me?

5. How do I remove the barriers?

6. What resources will I need to get started?

7. What resources do I have?

Answers to Act on:

8. What isn't working?

9. What is working?

10. What's the next step?

To do List:

Step 3

May

Step 4

Made a searching and fearless moral inventory of ourselves.

~ *Alcoholics Anonymous*

HERO

My dearest Jacob,

I awoke insanely early this morning, for reasons I still don't understand, and as I lay in bed wide away, I realized something; I don't need a man in my life, I NEED a hero.

I need a hero who is strong enough to hold me in his arms and make all the bad stuff go away; a hero who does the "sleeping dance" with me, where when we are sleeping together and I roll away, he rolls to me and when he rolls away, I roll to him; and when he rises to go to the bathroom I fidget in my sleep until he returns. I need a hero who matches me breath for breath, who makes me feel safe, who I fit in his body hug from head to toes, and who whispers in his sleep, "Are you my girl?". I need a hero who loves my hair and figures out where to put it all so we can be close; oh, and who can laugh when things in the bedroom don't go quite as planned. :)

I need a hero who can give me the special kiss, one long one followed by three short ones, our special code for "I love you"; who is strong enough to give me the five minute kiss or place his hand gently to my face and give me the kiss that makes me whisper "wow!". I need a hero whose words, "Good night, sweetheart," make me whole.

I need a hero who is gentle enough to play with my hair giving me comfort; who can wrestle in bed and make me giddy; and who calls out in the dark, "Are you okay?" when he hears me kick something. I need a hero who loves my Ali, who plays with her, sings to her, calls her his "girlfriend" and talks to her on the phone when she misses him.

I need a hero who wakes up in the morning and comes looking through the house for me and when he finds me, he smiles with relief that I am there; a hero who is brave enough to admit I make him smile so much it hurts or that he needs me to make him feel safe too; a hero who calls me in the middle of the night because he wants to come and see me for no other reason than just to see me, just to be with me; and a hero who wants to make me happy and content, and can do that by just being in the same room with me and breathing. I need a hero whose eyes light up when he sees me; and makes mine do the same.

Oh, and I need a hero who is smart; smart enough to take my ideas and make them better; smart enough to know how to stop my tirades in their tracks and make me smile doing it; and smart enough to teach me all the things I need to know to be a good person by being my example.

I need a hero who is funny cuz he tells corny jokes, laughs with me at the stupidest commercials, and can see the silly things in life; a hero who replies "Really?" with a lilt in his voice when he is surprised; and who never ceases to make me laugh when I least feel like doing it.

I need a hero I can trust to fix me food that I can eat, who keeps his house cleaner than mine, who loves to do the laundry, whose cologne excites me, whose candles make me feel cozy, and whose fabric softener doesn't make me sneeze. I need a hero who turns off the light when it's not being used, puts a trash bag in the waste can, fills his empty coffee mug with water when he puts it in the sink, and gets me a soft blanket when I lay on the sofa or coffee when he gets his. Oh, and doesn't mind when stray strands of my hair stays on the sofa, the pillows, wherever.

I need a hero who is kind not harsh but supportive; a hero who is on my side, who believes in me; a hero who is brave enough to tell me he is proud of me, that he thinks I am amazing, and who loves my writing instead of ridicules it. I need a hero who doesn't criticize me, ask me to change, or tell me what to do. A hero who is not afraid to let me see his tears when he cries over a friend's illness, as a show of appreciation for something I've done for him, or when he asks my forgiveness.

I need a hero who is incredibly handsome and charming; who regardless of what he is wearing, or isn't, can take my breath away; who makes me want to do nothing but kiss him all day and touch him all over; who is someone I can be proud to introduce to any and all I meet.

I need a hero who is spiritually connected to me; who's look can make my heart sing; who's touch can calm my soul; who's being can inspire me; and who's singing can make me cry.

I need a hero who is honorable, one whom I can respect; who always wants to do the right thing as he is able and stops me when I don't; who believes in the Almighty and strives to do as he thinks he should. I need a hero who connects with me on many levels; who gets that I am one way IN the bedroom, and a completely other way OUTSIDE the bedroom; and a hero who will keep my secrets safe.

I need all of these things to be better, to be the best I can be to carry out that which the Almighty has asked of me. I know it's a very big order.

Yes, Jacob, I need a hero ... and my hero ... is you. You are the wings that make me soar, the calm that keeps me safe, and you are everything I'd ever hoped to find in a man but was afraid I was asking for too much.

No, I don't know why I awoke so very early, perhaps it was just because the Almighty wanted me to tell you all of my heart's desires, what it is I need in my life, so that you would know.

Thank you for being my hero; I am very grateful.

With grace,
and admiration,
C

COMPETITION

I couldn't imagine competing with a beer can.

Needless to say, I equally couldn't imagine LOOSING.

Yet, as I sit here this morning, with my house chores done, taking a small break before grading papers, I realize that losing to a beer can is what my relationship with Jacob boils down to.

Sad that.

We brought out the best in each other and along the way learned how NOT to bring out the worst. We could have had life by the tail; but, the beer won. How can I compete with that?? I can't. So, I lose.

And what is it that I lose? Now there's a point I've not pondered before. Well, I lost the good stuff – the partnership, the friendship, the romance, and the bedroom fun. Along with it, I lost being ignored, lied to, cheated on, betrayed, and teased without mercy. I lost the endless temper tantrums, the running away, and the dashed hopes.

Some would say that it is a fair trade off. I'm not so sure.

My uncertainty comes in knowing that I saw the hand of G-d every step of the way; He was an integral part of our relationship; He guided my steps at every turn. This, of course, leads me to believe that this was the path G-d wanted me to take. I, of course, loved Jacob and was madly in love with him. Then, well, then the beer can enters the picture and all of Jacob's promises turned to lies; his actions didn't follow his words; and as much as he claimed he didn't want a relationship with me, his actions said much differently. He did exactly what he set out to do, prove that even if it was meant to be, we could mess it up and lose it. My fear is, if I saw the hand of G-d in this relationship and it doesn't work, then how can I trust what I see in the next one? I can't.

So here I sit, with my third cup of coffee, lighting one of too many cigarettes for the day and … wondering … now what??

It's clear to me that there is no other for me; that I am still to continue waiting for him; and that in the meantime, I'm to be working on other aspects of my life. How so? You ask.

Well, let me put it to you this way, no one else has stepped up to the plate. I have no men calling me, sending me text messages, or inviting me to dinner. Yes, I've had three guys in three weeks be nice to me, give me compliments; but, it goes no further. I've had a couple men e-mail me with their stupid letters void of correct grammar and hinting at "adult" entertainment.

But, I want more.

Jacob showed me the more I want; and I'm guessing that until such time as that more is available to me I will … wait. I don't sit by idly waiting for him to call or come by, mind you. No, I fill my days with taking good care of myself, helping others as I can, doing the best I can at my job; and finding joy as it occurs. This waiting thing isn't easy for me; but I'm praying it will be worth it.

I'm also hoping I get a second chance; and I'm really hoping he's won his battle with the beer can. If he hasn't we both will lose.

SOLUTIONS

The solution to the morning after: shake awake; quick kiss; "Have a great day!"; and leave so fast you don't close the door behind you.

It was exactly what Jacob did.

He had figured out what I could not: how to face the morning after so all would be right in his world. There was no awkward conversation, no love making, no chance of disappointments, and certainly no facing of future plans. It was perfect. For him.

I smell his cologne lightly in the house, find some comfort in that he DID kiss me goodbye before he left, and wonder if this really was a ***good*** solution; or just ***a*** solution.

As I sit here on the front patio, dressed only in his white terrycloth bathrobe, having my first coffee of the day, listening to the animals about me, and realizing it really is waaay too early to be up on a Sunday morning, I realize something else: maybe it *is* the things left unsaid, undone, left alone, or run away from that do matter.

If Friday was the day to set the standard for the good days, than Saturday was the day to set the standard for the average days. I had asked him in the morning if he remembered our conversations the night before; which he said he did.

I knew he wasn't "feeling well", as he put it, clearly the beer and the golf the day before were taking their toll; and yet, I spent the day trying to get his attention; trying to get the time to discuss in further detail the two issues he had agreed to the night before; him helping me with my writing career, and the loaning of the money for my phone bill and groceries.

It didn't happen. Fact was, every time I got near him he made it clear for whatever reason, he didn't want me there. To add insult to injury, every time I backed away, he didn't follow. A girl can only take so much rejection; so shortly after we got up for the day I sat near him and gently said, "I know sometimes when I don't feel well, all I really want is to be left alone." He moaned and tilted his head back as if to say, "Oh, no, not this!" I continued, by saying, "I know you've got to leave early tomorrow, and you've got services tonight, would you like me to leave?"

The look of shock on his face was answer enough, but his words of reassurance in wanting me to stay was an added bonus. So, I did stay; and went to the grocer and did some errands and I thought again, all would be right in our world.

But it wasn't; time was slipping away, and he was running away; through ignoring me; his cutting or snide remarks; and his meanness which only showed through when he was sober I was getting a bit worried.

When I'd finished going to the grocer, I stopped and picked us up lunch. Standing in the kitchen putting away the groceries we each fixed our plate (I only cringed a little at the huge amount of ketchup he put on his plate) and went into the living room. I sat on the sofa and set my plate on the coffee table. It was the coolest table I'd ever seen; the top came up and towards the sofa so it was the perfect height to use as a dinning room table. I patted the space next to me and said, "Come, sit by me." He shook his head no and just as regally as a king went to sit in his recliner. With great purpose he set his plate on the small table next to the recliner, settled into the chair, picked up the table and went to move it around to the front of the chair when the leg caught on the chair.

Just as slick as ice that plate fell onto the floor, landing upside down, and spewing ketchup across the very expensive carpeting. We jumped up and I grabbed some napkins, told him to get the stain remover and a wet cloth, and I began cleaning up the mess.

I put the food back on the plate, the plate back on the table, and gingerly begin to address the very large ketchup mess. As I'm taking care of the mess ... he is ... whining. "Why does this always happen to me?" he whined, pacing back and forth. "Why do I always have such bad luck?" he continued. Not helping clean up the mess, not taking ANY responsibility for the mess, he was just incessantly whining about it.

"Bad luck!?!" I screamed inside my head. "It wasn't BAD LUCK!! If you had sat next to me on the sofa, THIS wouldn't have happened." As I knelt on the floor, I couldn't help but wonder ... is this what living with him is really like?? Does he let his pride dictate his actions and then negate the responsibility of clean up to others? I couldn't say anything to him; I couldn't afford to piss him off; I still needed the favor he'd promised the night before.

Instead, I finished cleaning up; washed my hands; went back to the sofa and tried to finish my meal. I say tried as watching him eat his food bathed in ketchup made me lose my appetite; it was if he suddenly had also forgotten his manners.

By about eight o'clock I finally started the conversation I'd been trying to have all day; the one in which he agreed to loan me the money for my phone bill. To which he abruptly got up and went back into the house, stating another of his mindless "favorite" television shows was on and he just had to watch it. I let him go and just sat there, feeling again, rejected. Ten minutes later I walked in the house, just as he was getting a call from another woman, a so-called "friend" who has cancer; to which he grabbed his cigarettes and walked outside to take the call.

He came back after his show was off.

I sat and listened to him tell me how alone she was with all of her family around her; I could relate to this as I felt alone sitting next to him. I listened to him tell me how he had discussed her with his best friend on the golf course the day before. I realized how he could sit outside and chat with her and never once tell her, or anyone else, that I was there. Fact is, there was no one in his life who knew about me; and there were few people in my life that didn't know about him.

When he'd finished telling me all about her, her condition, how he couldn't figure out why the Almighty had brought her into his life, and had resolved the issue for the night, I couldn't help but feel ... well ... jealous. I, mean, come on, I am human. Here was a woman he had cried over as I held him; a woman whose calls he takes in the sweltering heat and negates the show he'd left me to watch; a woman he had volunteered to be tested for a bone marrow transplant; and a woman he had never even met; yet, I meant so little that his words to me were hollow, his promises empty, and not a single person in his life knew I existed? Who am I kidding when I think we have something?

The subject changed to what to have for dinner and ended with us deciding if he paid for it, I'd go get some dinner. Seeing no better time for it, I broached the subject of the phone bill, saying he didn't have to answer me now, but to think about it and when I got back, we'd discuss it. The look on his face was proof enough that he didn't recall the conversation; didn't realize the deal he'd made, and was in no position to keep the deal; or worse yet, he did remember but was now reneging on it. Some of his comments throughout the day would point to the latter, not the former.

I passed it off as no big thing and left. But, it was a big thing. I'd taken comfort in believing him that the deal would be honored and now it wasn't. The subject was not mentioned again. I was quiet for the rest of the evening, ignoring him, being distant, walking away from him; basically giving him the same treatment as he'd given me minus the cutting, snide remarks. He didn't notice, or he didn't care; either way, I was on my own ... again.

I was on the back deck when he came and told me he was going to bed giving my knee a pat; and if I joined him fine, if I didn't, equally as fine; it was up to me. I joined him several minutes later, and he ... well ... ignored me. I rolled over and just lay there for a few minutes; he asked me if I was okay, I said I was fine before getting up and going back on the deck. I didn't know what to do ... he was running away from me ... again; but now it was in the bedroom. This time, though, I knew it wasn't because of anything I'd done.

When I got back in bed, I rolled over close to him and said, "I can take you running away from me in the house, but I can't take it in the bedroom." He moaned in anticipation of my words. I mentioned his taking her call and my tone was one of disappointment.

"Please, baby," he whispered, "I so don't want to go there, not now. I just want to get some sleep as I've a long day tomorrow."

He pulled me in close, and gave me one of his good kisses. I rolled over. "Don't you go turning your back on me," he said, following me.

As we lay in what had become our favorite spooning position, I said, "Can I ask you something?"

"Yes, baby," he said. It was there – the tone of voice that said all I wanted to hear – that we were okay. It was the voice he used when we connected and I was ever so glad he was using it now.

"Never mind," I whispered, "You've already answered it." It's a nice feeling, laying there, feeling safe, and wanted, and ... dare I say ... loved.

But, the feelings didn't last long; and I became restless, up and down to the bathroom, going out for the final smoke of the night; the broken deal and the ramifications of it weighed heavy on my mind. Coupled with his actions of how he perceived us, I was beside myself.

I couldn't help but wonder, would there always be something or someone who was more important in his life than … me? The answer slapped my face; yes, at least for now.

I take comfort in knowing that it is I who is sleeping in his bed; I he will think of when he fixes the food I got him; and I whose hair he finds in the strangest of places. It is a cold comfort and it smacks of me somehow fulfilling the role of "the other woman". There are no pictures of me at his home, and he'd just recently taken hers' off the refrigerator door. There is always an excuse why I'm not invited to meet his family; or his friend's, or even the party being thrown by his bank. There is never a time when he discusses me with anyone; or tells anyone I'm with him. His words, written in an anger induced retaliation, "Why do you think I am never with you in public?" speaks volumes of what I don't want to hear. I feel like I am somehow his dirty little secret; an embarrassment to him; somehow, again, not worthy of him.

He told me Friday night that things were going to change; he held me close and pleaded with me, "Please, don't give up on me. I'm a good man … I'm learning … things will get better… baby steps." We made promises of never getting to the point of ripping each other apart, and agreed we'd had some really rough patches, but there was the hope that what we had really would get better.

Sadly, it's not enough. I'd been down that road of hoping too many times; and just as many finding it was a dead-end with us.

Maybe he has the right idea; maybe it is best to run away, and think, and then come back to the issue when you've got your ducks in a row. And maybe the chance we take is it will be too late when we are ready to come back.

I don't know if he heard me call out "Goodbye," to him as he left this morning. I really hope he did.

NEW STUFF

What ever happened to brown?

Come to think of it, what happened to red too?

In my box of sixty-four crayons I have: tan, Indian red, bittersweet, burnt orange, burnt sienna, not to be confused with raw sienna; but, the brown is missing. I'm not saying it's not there; just that it must be hiding.

As to the red, well, I have: maroon, fuchsia, magenta, , wild strawberry, brick red, mulberry, and red violet, not to be confused (I suppose) with violet red; but, no red. Perhaps the red has gone missing with the brown.

Now, before you start wondering why a grown woman even HAS a box of sixty-four crayons, let alone is concerned with what colors are in the box, I'll tell you that there are few things in life that can calm the nerves and get you in a 'good place' faster than a box of crayons and a coloring book.

Seriously, except for blowing soap bubbles, there are few things which can evoke the certain magic that happens when you stop and rest for a bit like coloring. It's as if in coloring you are nurturing the inner child who keeps getting lost in all the day-to-day adult activities that we have to do. I want to find her again; nurture her more this new year; revel in the joy she experiences; and protect her from those … unworthy.

It's hard to do this sometimes; it's hard to let the wall come down and let her shine through as she's been hurt so many times before; even now she cries for the mistreatment she's gotten from Jacob; the loss she feels, the emptiness which has engulfed her.

Yet, there is comfort in the strangest of fashions.

While at services yesterday I read something; and G-d said: "I'm hiding; and no one wants to find me!"

I know what that's like; it hurts; especially when you do, and do, and then do some more, and the one you are doing for discounts your gifts, tosses away your blessings; and discards you.

It must be hard for the Almighty to do so much for so many, only to be tossed aside when the crisis is over and all is right in their world. It must be ever so painful for Him to show those who choose blindness the good things He has in store for them and they continue to choose blindness. What tolerance must He posses to be able to continually go back to those He's helped and show them the righteous path knowing that they probably won't take it? How very infinite His patience to try just ONE more time, to do just ONE more thing, to hope just ONE more time that this will be the act that make the non-believers, believe.

I just wonder, do you think He'll share his crayons? I really hope so.

NONE

It was just a form.

So, why did writing the word “None” make my hands shake?

Through miracles of miracles, I found that I had received a full scholarship for my Judaism classes; this was last week Friday when the whole day was filled with miracles. As my meeting with the Rabbi was to be on this coming Monday morning, I figured filling out the form now would save me some rush time later.

It was a simple enough form; one page, nothing too personal and rather direct. Yet, when I turned the page over to fill out the back side, the first question stopped me in my tracks. “Partner’s name”. That’s all it said; two simple words; the sole reason for the question to determine class size.

With shaky hands, I wrote, “None”. It was just as simple a response to a very simple question. So what’s with the drama, the shaky hands, the feeling of a rock in the pit of my stomach?

Because it was true. I had no partner in this endeavor; it was just me ... and the Almighty. I had no partner in any other endeavor either. As Jacob and I were again in the off-position, though it looked like there was some hope (however slim) of us getting to the “on” position, I couldn’t ask him to take this class with me. He was, after all, a Catholic by conversion.

I guess the reason for the drama was, quite simply, because I WANTED a partner; I wanted someone to enjoy with me this phase of my life; well, I wanted a partner to enjoy all the phases in my life. Yet, that was not to be ... right now.

I read in my CoDA book a passage that said, in essence, that we need to give others time and space and emotional freedom to adjust, to change, to accept things, issues, and emotions. They are right, we do; fact is that is where Jacob and I are right now; giving ourselves some time to see if our relationship is something we want, or something we want to let go of.

I would like to believe this time is a good place we are in; that the time alone will give us the space we need to do all that we need to do; and that at some point we will be together in a personal relationship which encompasses all that we have to offer each other. But, I have my doubts.

May

There is much on my plate today; I've done an incredible amount of catch up work with the flat, and my cat, and cleaning in general to even include the toilet, the tub and a few windows. I've still got homework to do and prep work for my teaching classes which begin on Monday. Yet, there is still this period of time when my thoughts turn to him; to us. And, I smile.

Yes, the form may dictate that the answer be "None"; but, that's just for today. The Almighty is always with me and perhaps, just perhaps, this is a journey for just Him and I. I sure would like to think so. ☺

SUMMARY

Did you see a parallel to an issue in your own life? The following ten questions may help you gain new perspective on how to manage it.

Questions to ponder:

1. Is this issue bigger than me?

2. What is my part in resolving the issue?

3. Is now the right time?

4. What's stopping me?

5. How do I remove the barriers?

6. What resources will I need to get started?

7. What resources do I have?

Answers to Act on:

8. What isn't working?

9. What is working?

10. What's the next step?

To do List:

Step 4

June

Step 5

Admitted to God, to ourselves, and to another human being the exact nature of our wrongs.

~ *Alcoholics Anonymous*

TRUST

My Dearest Jacob,

Trust -- hurt -- betrayal; odd words for you to use against me.

How many times have you hurt me by breaking my trust and betraying me? Friday night is a perfect example; you tell me not to worry, that you can help me; yet, when it comes down to the wire, you don't.

I was very hurt over that betrayal; as it was just one of many. You running away from me on Saturday, not having time to work on my things that we had discussed on Friday night; all added to the fire of my hurt. Not to mention that you walked away from me to watch a TV show; just to take her call outside and miss the show completely. Your priorities were her, TV, and then ... me. To add even more, you sit and tell me how you and Mark have discussed her ... but yet, there is NO ONE in your life that knows about me; and at every turn, you make sure that I am excluded from anything in your life. Again, I was hurt realizing this.

Trust -- I believed you, time and time and time again; only to find that you were not as good as your word; you wouldn't call when you said you would, you wouldn't carry through on tentative plans. And these actions would hurt me a great deal; but, yet, I was the one to have to understand the situation. Telling me your actions this morning were actually a comfort to me -- I thought maybe you were running away from me ... again.

Each time, I would forgive you; though at times I'd cry for days, I'd swear I'd never see you again; still, when you'd call, I'd accept or invite you over, or I'd open the door; because I ... care ... for you. Although I can rarely trust your word, or count on you for anything more than right this minute; I forgave you without you even asking. You are a good man and I see this goodness.

However, you've said the most horrible of things to me, even on Saturday your snide and cutting comments hurt me; they were said for no reason that I can think of but that you were uncomfortable with me being there. Many of the things you've said to me are hurtful; but still I forgave you, without reservations.

I am in no way justifying my actions for getting into your email account and reading the emails you are sending to other women for I concur they were deplorable. However, I found myself in a strange situation today; and my only thoughts were of protecting you from someone who scared you even more than I do. I thought of protecting the ones you care about even more than you care about me. Strange that you say the way for me to hurt you is to contact them; the reason is ... they don't know about me; they think they are your one and only; they are the one you love. And they are right. In a moment of weakness, I tried to protect you from someone else and it has cost me dearly. I would NEVER contact them. That's not me, or who I am; though I doubt you believe that. The reason is, I would never deliberately do something to hurt you; no matter how angry or hurt I was.

I've given up all my markers as I couldn't take the chance of it scaring you even more. Strange that you are hurt by my actions, when you are telling me that you care more for them ... then you do for me. Have you ANY idea of how much that hurts me?? Of course not, for they are all more important to you ... than I am; they are more worthy of you than I am. I am the one who stands by you, helps you in every way that I can, proves my loyalty and devotion to you every day. I am the one held in the closet, hidden from public view -- as you said -- you just wanted to lay me and forget me, as that was why we've never been seen together in public -- not even to go to Wal-Mart. My only mistake was an error in judgment.

I give you my word, there is no need for threats against me, as I truly am a good a faithful servant of G-d and I had a moment of weakness in which I stumbled. (I pray He will show mercy on me, especially if you don't.) A mistake that I will never make again as the pain is too great. I ask only that you forgive me ... that you try to trust me again ... as this is the only time I've ever given you to doubt me. I treat you and your things as if they were mine; I am careful with them; respect them; and treat them with the utmost of care. I have proven this as well, time and again.

You ask for time; I think we both need some time ... to think, to question our own feelings or lack thereof. I am truly sorry for my actions ... and not for the reason you think. Yes, I did invade your privacy and that was wrong -- though my intentions were honorable. I am sorry for my actions for they proved to me just how very much you love others and just how very little you care for me.

This pain above all is my greatest punishment. You are more afraid of me telling them about me ... then you are about ... us.

I seek only your forgiveness; perhaps this time apart will either prove we have something worth working on or something to let go; perhaps it may make us stronger, I wish it would. I ask only that you do not TELL THEM what I have done for to do so, per Temple law, I will need to seek their forgiveness as well. Whoever you tell, I will need to make restitution to for my error.

May we both find ... understanding and peace.

With grace,
limited as it is sometimes,
C

LOGIC IN THE ILLOGICAL

Jacob left; I quit writing.

Where's the logic there?

I will admit that Jacob and our relationship had become the focal point of too many of my writings; but, he wasn't all of it. Jacob was not at the heart of all of my writings; he wasn't the inspiration behind them; he was just the catalyst for the lessons I was learning.

So, um, why did I stop writing? Okay, maybe STOP isn't the right word; perhaps slowly-dwindle-down-to-fewer-than-normal would be a good word, if it is a word at all. Was it because I no longer had anything to say? Was it because I had finished learning all of my lessons? Was it because maybe, just maybe I'm not the writer I thought I was. Or horror of all horrors, was it because my gift of writing was taken away?

How about: none of the above?

The logic of it all was simple – I don't know. I had found myself in a dark place; normally when I'm there, I'll write myself into a better mood; I'll express myself as a point of therapy; I'll even try to figure out the lesson the Almighty is trying to teach me.

Yet, lately, that hasn't been the case. It's not so much that I don't have the time to write; as I do. It's more that I didn't have the desire. My morning routine was simple: get up, make coffee, feed the cat, make the bed, check my e-mails, talk to the Almighty; write; get on with my day. The routine hasn't changed except for the writing bit.

It makes good sense to be grateful for that which the Almighty has given us; and He has given me a great deal to be grateful for this last month. It also makes sense to wisely use the gifts that he gives us. I haven't been doing that as I've been neglecting my writing.

If I believe all of the self-help, recovery, program books the logic would dictate that I am:

- Right where I am supposed to be,
- Doing what I am supposed to be doing,
- Learning the lessons I am presented with so I don't need to learn them again,
- Walking in the grace of the Almighty.

Oddly enough, I do believe all of that. But, I find that there is a piece or two missing. I go through my days believing that I am taking one step forward on my journey of self-discovery; yet, I go through them ... alone. I am in awe of the opportunities the Almighty has presented me with and do my part to take advantage of them; but there are few to share them with. I find that moments of true joy are coming at a faster pace, yet, it doesn't fill the emptiness of having the one I love in my life.

And still ... I cry for, I long to have, I want with all my being that which is not available to me. The logic in this life doesn't track; it doesn't make sense that all the other areas of my life are exploding with goodness and blessings, and yet, I am coloring my rainbows with a shade of gray for the missing of the final piece.

I had my hopes, my dreams, my visions from the Almighty; and they are now gone; which leaves a hole in my soul.

I'd like to believe that there is a lesson in here somewhere; I'd like to believe that it is the same one I've been trying to learn all along – let go and let G-d. I guess it just may take a little more time, and pain, and aloneness for me to learn it.

Then again, you can't choose the one you love. You can, however, choose to let them go and love them anyway.

Perhaps it would be wise to remember, when we try to look for the logic in the illogic of emotions, we may just find the hope.

DENIAL

It's been nearly two weeks since I've written something of substance.

Just about the same time since I've seen Jacob.

The correlation did not go unnoticed by me; though I wish it had. Now, I'm not saying he is my muse, my inspiration, nor anything else; what I am saying is that, well, like my daily writings, I do miss him.

We had gotten to the point where we both decided we needed some space to determine if we wanted to continue the relationship or let it go; it was the weekend of my Miracle Friday; my life will never be the same.

Two weeks ago today set me on the most amazing of journeys which led to this week being the beginning of a whole different life; the life I asked the Almighty for, the life He granted me.

It will take some time to settle into this new life, but this is the overview: I got the assistant professor's position, so I teach every afternoon at a university I love, doing what I do best, with students who are wonderful; with my first solid paycheck in years. I got the scholarship so Tuesday nights are my Judaism classes; through grace I found Codependence Anonymous, so my meetings are Wednesday nights; I've Temple on Friday nights; the Ethical Society on Sunday mornings; this is my last week of classes for my MBA before my research project; and to top it all off, I've a new client coming in to put me on solid financial ground. Every step of the way, I see the Almighty's hand.

But, He didn't stop there. Then there's Jacob, with two days of snafus of sorts; Monday he called to accuse me of writing his ex-girlfriend an e-mail; which ended with him saying he was sorry he said he wanted me to leave, but his phone cut out and he didn't call me back. And Wednesday ... well, that was a night of the most unusual sorts.

So it was, after my CoDA meeting, I thought long and hard about the letting go process; the detachment issue. And as I was walking up the stairs to my flat, I said out loud, "Okay, Almighty, it's up to you. If you want it to work between Jacob and I, it will; if you don't, it won't. Either way, I'll be good with it."

Upon arriving home, I see Jacob's sent me an e-mail saying to never contact him again. That was at 7:08. I checked my messages and there were TWO messages from him -- at 7:42, and 7:52 -- the last one was so long it got cut off. BOTH of them saying I HAD to call him tonight or ELSE.

What was truly odd about the situation is the timing; at the exact same time as he was calling my house, I was sitting at my CoDA meeting and had this overwhelming urge to let him go -- it was at this point I decided to turn him over to the Almighty; to let Him make of us what He will; yet, didn't express these thoughts until I arrived home. Although Jacob's last message said he'd called my cell phone and it went from a quick ring to a busy signal so he didn't know if my cell was cut off or not; I knew my cell was working as I kept looking it for the clock function and the bars showed full service. It was as if the Almighty didn't want me to get his call at that time.

This was the second time he'd made contact with me this week, and the thought which kept running through my mind was this: even though he was calling to complain about something, it was almost as if he was using this situation as an excuse TO call me. There was an underlying tone to his voice, one of ... pleasure; one saying he was happy just to talk to me regardless of the situation.

I gathered my courage about me, and called him -- he didn't answer the phone – so I left him a message. Then, I wrote him an e-mail saying I was confused. Right after I sent it -- he called me; saying he didn't get my messages; and that I HAD to hear him out. Bottom line, he said we **had** a good relationship with the implication I destroyed it.

Well, I asked him, "When? When did we have a great relationship? Cuz the first night we met was a Sunday; you stayed the night at my place; Tuesday I spent the night at your place: and Saturday was the end of four days of silence." He didn't want to address this subject at all; so, as was his custom, he skipped it.

I told him he had been running away from me from the git go -- how scared he was -- how he accused me of moving too fast, but he was leading the parade; how every aspect of our relationship was geared to what HE wanted and that it was up to ME to change to meet those needs, to accept those boundaries, and to be good with it.

Yet, it was through discussing this with my CoDA sponsor that she said something I'd been blind to: Jacob was in denial. But, it was a denial I'd never considered before. I was of the mindset that "denial" meant seeing all the good, and DENYING the bad; she made me realize it can just as easily mean seeing all the bad and DENYING the good!

This was a type of denial I'd never experienced personally, but upon reflection, had come up against several times with several men in my life. Wasn't my fight to prove myself to them, to show them the value in what we had, to do something – anything – to convince them what we had was good, nothing more than fighting their wall of denial? I'm beginning to see how it was.

Putting a label on a problem helps a great deal; it relieves some of the stress in trying to figure out what is wrong, it helps set a plan of action, and it gives us a new set of tools to work with. It's a comfort to know what our place is in a relationship even if it means we have no place; to realize we are not responsible for nor can we control the actions of another, as that's their job; and to realize the best thing we can do is leave it alone and let the Almighty do what He does best.

It does not, however, provide warmth, comfort, and security in the wee hours of the morning as we sleep alone.

A MATTER OF TRUST

Today I realized I'm having some major trust issues.

The problem is the person I'm not trusting is ... me.

It's easy to say that you don't trust your parents, your boyfriend, your friends; but how do you NOT trust yourself? Even more importantly, how do you get back that trust once you've lost it?

Trust is one issue which is built on past history or future plans. If every time someone tells you they are going to do something, and they don't do it, the next time they say they are going to, you'll not trust that they will.

Unless, that is, something changes.

Thursday afternoon I got my paycheck stub – as my checks are direct deposited – and even though I knew that this one should be higher than the previous ones, I wasn't prepared for HOW high. Because of this surprise I immediately believed that I was reading it wrong; that I had somehow made a mistake in my math; and that for some reason I couldn't trust what I was reading. I refused to get excited about it, for I just knew that I was reading it wrong and that the money wouldn't be as high as the stub said it was.

I spent the rest of the evening rechecking my math; pulling out the contract and double checking my figures; changing my method of figuring it out; and then ended up calling the HR person in the morning to make sure the number was right.

But, my own mistrust didn't stop there. Of course not, it had to bleed over into Friday morning. Shortly after I called the HR person and confirmed the amount was correct, I started to send Jacob an e-card. Half way through, I suddenly thought I should call a friend of mine to make sure that I was saying the right thing and doing it for all the right reasons. I stopped short when I realized that SHE didn't know him better than I did and really could do little but either talk me out of this decision or confirm that it was the right one.

As if it my mistrust was limited, I found myself biting my tongue when I handed in my rent check. I wanted to scream at the office manager, "CASH IT TODAY!!" Why? Because I didn't trust that the money would be there if they waited.

But, it would be there. My check was twice what my previous checks were; and nearly twice what the rent check I'd just handed her was. I hadn't overspent what was already in my account, and hadn't even touched the new deposit.

So, what's up with all the mistrust? Changes.

My life has changed so quickly, so drastically in the last two months, that I don't know if I'm afoot or horseback. All the endings and all the new beginnings have challenged who I think I am; and in the midst of all of these changes I'm swimming in a pool of ... uncertainty.

The waters of my life are starting to settle, but it's the bits around the edges where what once was, is no longer; where what I once did was acceptable, it, too, is no longer; and who I once was ... is not who I am today.

And I am ... frightened. It is not so much that these changes are bad changes; they are not. They are all good changes, but still, they ARE changes.

With the fear comes the mistrust; I was afraid that the money the stub reflected wasn't real, hence, I would be disappointed when I found out the error. But, it was real.

I was afraid sending Jacob an e-card would destroy what we have. But, we don't have anything, and so there could be no damage to the relationship.

I was afraid my check wouldn't clear because past practice had me cutting my finances so close to the bone that there was a chance that it wouldn't. But, this time, it would clear easily.

Normally I not only deal well with changes, but, I relish them – strive for them – instigate them – and am bored when things get stagnant. I roll with the best of them when it comes to dealing with sudden upheavals in my life; but, now, well, now I'm not as sure of myself as I have been.

I need to trust the new things in my life, to realize that I finally have things that no one can take away from me; that I can't lose. I will always have my MBA, my certificate of completion for my Judaism classes, and the teaching experience I've gained. I will always have a place to lay my head and a car to drive – as long as the Almighty helps me make my payments. ☺

But above all, I will always have ... me. The only constants in my life are me and my belief in the Almighty; those two things have never faltered, have never failed me. Though my faith has at times wavered, it has only been for short periods. What I really, really need, is to believe in ... me.

There are many reasons why I don't believe in me, too many reasons, too much pain, too many times when others tried to break that belief. Yet, I realize that all in all, when it came down to the wire, I made it happen, I did what I needed to do, and I succeeded. I didn't do it alone, but I did do it with just me and the Almighty.

There's no better team than me and the Almighty. I know He will help me gain the trust and the faith that He has in me. He will see me through these changes, will allow me to become excited at the new opportunities, and will show me that if I only believe in me a fraction of what He believes in me that all really will be right in my world. I need to realize, when our trust in ourselves is diminished, we need only look at how G-d trusts us to get it back. I just wish Jacob would trust me; but, if I can't, how can I expect him to?

I'm good with working on this.

SUMMARY

Did you see a parallel to an issue in your own life? The following ten questions may help you gain new perspective on how to manage it.

Questions to ponder:

1. Is this issue bigger than me?

2. What is my part in resolving the issue?

3. Is now the right time?

4. What's stopping me?

5. How do I remove the barriers?

6. What resources will I need to get started?

7. What resources do I have?

Answers to Act on:

8. What isn't working?

9. What is working?

10. What's the next step?

To do List:

Step 5

July

Step 6

Were entirely ready to have God remove all these defects of character.

~ *Alcoholics Anonymous*

CROSSROADS

My Dearest Jacob,

I awoke this morning confused, concerned, and really questioning whether or not yesterday morning really happened at all. Did I really wake up with you, spend a wonderful day with you, and leave feeling like we had taken some real steps in progress? I was talking to the Almighty, and was really seeking some answers to my own questions, my own doubts about you, my own fears about my feelings, and whether or not I should continue on this journey with you.

The enclosed was His answer -- it wasn't mine, not really of my own creation, more like I was the vessel and He was the creator. (This sounds about right in more ways than one.) I thought it was His answer to me; I realize after reading it several times, it was the answer to both of us.

This is probably the most honest e-mail I've ever sent you; there are no games, no carefully chosen words used to garner a response, no heartfelt pleas for your attention; it's just me, being painfully honest with you. I see a great deal in you; your gifts are priceless to me; and when we are good, well, I couldn't ask for anything better in life for I am at my best. Perhaps that is the meaning of soul mate; I have no idea.

I'm on my own journey too; I've lots of work to do, many things yet to accomplish; I have many answers to find, decisions to make, and improvements to set in motion. But, I'm honest enough with myself to know, I can't do it alone. If that makes me weak or needy or undesirable in some way, so be it. Yet, it may also be the way the Almighty intended; that we each have things to do, but need another to do them.

When your wall is down and you are truly with me, I find in you the one person in my life to date who makes me better, who makes me feel safe in the middle of the night, who touches my soul and inspires me. You are proud of me and that really did bring me to tears; you think I am amazing; you love my writing nearly as much as I do; when you hold me in your arms, you can make all the bad stuff in the world go away; and, well, when you kiss me, when you touch me, all is right in the world. You give me that which I cannot give myself. That's all I need.

You and your gifts are all I need to be the best I can be; they are the tools the Almighty has sent me to do the work He has asked of me to do. There is no other who has your gifts, they are uniquely your own; they may not be good enough for you or the others in your life, but to me, they are priceless. To the world you may be just one person; but to me, you are the world. I understand that you and your gifts are locked in your own prison cell; as mine are as well; but I pray, I sincerely pray that there will come a day when you will allow me the honor of unlocking your cell as I will allow you to unlock mine. For then, and only then, can we both give the world the gifts that the Almighty has given us to share.

With grace,
and love,
C

HOLES

I feel like I need to write today.

But, I've no idea what I'm supposed to write about.

As I sit here there's a song playing on the CD player called "Holes" by Rascal Flats; I've done my to-do list and started some of the things on it; and I've plenty more to do. I talked to the Almighty this morning and thanked him for all the good stuff in my life and asked for some help on the not-so-good stuff. I've also talked to two of my good friends this morning – one is just thrilled that it's her day off; the other is wallowing in the overwhelming joy of finally talking to his parents after a four-year absence.

And I'm trying very, very hard to NOT think about Jacob. I'm not doing it very well. I know all the logical arguments telling me to think about him will only push him farther away; how I need to forget about him and work on me; and how this minor act is not getting me to where I belong; AND to do anything at all will only spoil the soup. But, all in all, it's just hard realizing how long it's been since I've talked to him and not knowing what's going to happen; is the game over? Are we just taking a break? Am I making more of this than it was? Does it matter??? Therein lies the real crux of the situation ... does all that I did for him, for us, mean ... nothing?

I don't know.

I do know there is a hole in my heart and my soul where he used to live. I do know that G-d has my best interest at heart and is working on His plan for me. And above all I do know whatever happens, happens and there is very little I can do about it.

But, there are moments, like right now, when my thoughts turn to what we had and I mourn the loss of it all. Perhaps I'm jumping the gun a bit; perhaps, just perhaps as the sun has just come out from a long morning of rain and storms, that there is hope for us – to be better than we could ever had imagined it to be; that G-d in His infinite wisdom and grace has provided us each this time of getting our lives together so when we do get back together we will exceed our wildest dreams.

Or maybe I'm just the queen of denial.

Either way, I still have this … hole. But I'm guessing 'tis better to fill it with hope than despair; for then, and only then, can I get on with all the other stuff on my to-do list and take excellent care of myself. ☺

NEW THINGS; OLD MEMORIES

My bed looks strange to me.

Sadly, it's more than just the new quilt.

And so it was ... today was the day I decided to change ... my bedding. Yes, I've washed it regularly!! But, although I have a closet full of bedding, I haven't really CHANGED what was on the bed. It quickly became a habit to take the bedding off – wash them all – then, put them back on.

The sheets were the ones I bought two weeks before I met Jacob; the first comforter was the one I bought with my ex-husband; and the top quilt -- well -- as it was, it was nearly identical to the one Jacob had on his bed. I always thought it odd that we'd chose the same type of bedding independently of each other. I decided to make this change shortly after waking up this morning and realizing I slept on the parlor bed more times than not. Fact is since I've met Jacob I've not slept in my own bed every night for a solid week straight.

I had vowed to only share my bed with the man I loved; my forever man; and I shared it only with Jacob. As it is, every single time I get into bed I remember what it was like when he was there; holding me, sleeping in the spooning position, his breath on the back of my neck, and the comfort I found there. Some nights I can deal with him being gone; but most nights, well, I can't.

I got an e-mail today about how things don't change, people do; and I thought about all the changes I've made; so, on impulse I read another from one of those dating sites, and updated my site listing. Thinking this was the change I should make, I promptly hid the listing after I'd finished because I felt so ... bad about it. It was as if I'd stopped waiting for Jacob to come back, as if I'd stopped trusting G-d, and was going to try something new. As much as I thought I wanted to, I found I couldn't go down that road.

So it was my friend Mary came over, we had a lovely brunch at First Watch; and I could feel Tuesday Morning calling my name. Having a bit of disposable income, we both agreed it was free to look. And then, well, then I found this lovely French quilt -- on sale, no less; and I had the money to buy it. But the thought of changing my bedding from sheets and a quilt that was of Jacob... well ... it stopped me. This did not go unnoticed by my friend and she gently said, "It's beautiful and maybe, just maybe it's ... time." She was right and I bought it.

She gave me the strength, the courage if you will, to realize how changing the bedding didn't mean I'm no longer waiting for Jacob; I'm just trying to find a way to cope with sleeping ... alone. She even helped me turn the futon and change all the bedding. I needed the help for I fear I would not have actually done it without her.

I hope changing the bedding will help; I pray there will be a time when I can actually sleep the whole night every night for a month in my own bed. I still believe Jacob will be back (G-d keeps telling me he will) and all will be as it should be; but in the meantime, I need to do what's right for me. I wish I could say I've done all of this without crying ... but I can't.

G-d's will be done.

CHANGING SEASONS

How can you care for me as you've only known me X amount of time?

That's the time argument I'm most familiar with hearing.

My stance has always been, "Don't discount what we have by the limited amount of time we've been together." In essence, "Time has nothing to do with it."

So, why is it, do you think, that every single day I wake up and tick off the days it's been since I've seen Jacob, since he's written me, or since I've written him? Is it because I'm wrong about time? Is it because time DOES matter? Or, is it just because I've never been in this situation where I've felt the need to wait for someone and had faith that waiting is the only way to get what I'm really wanting – a real relationship with him? Why is it that I give importance to the days/weeks/months that he is absent in my life as others discounted what we had because of the limited time we were together?

What does it matter if he comes back today, next week, next month or six months from now IF when he does come back we are both where we need to be to make the life we both want? It matters because I want it RIGHT NOW. It matters because I don't know how to feel or what to do or what to believe in the "Waiting Time". It matters because I feel like I have lost the most wonderful relationship I've ever had. It matters because I'm afraid I've lost something that I will never find with another and at this point I'm not even willing to try. It matters because I don't know that he IS coming back and I want to know. I want to make a decision about my life and I need to know if he is coming back to do so.

Ahhhh – there's the heart of the matter. I am depending on the actions of another to base decisions on in my life. Isn't that the definition of co-dependent? I don't know, but it sounds like it is.

I'm really rather frightened right now as it feels like I am on the edge of discovery and I'm not sure I want to go down this path. But – here I am, and so, let's go there.

I met Jacob in the winter of this year; we had something really good in the spring; it got better in the summer; and now, well if I take his "Take care!" statement as "Good bye" and his absence in my life as confirmation, then I guess we're over come the autumn.

All of my barriers came crashing down with him; I found myself "broken open", venerable, and wanting to take advantage of all the signs that said we were supposed to be together. And I thought the signs meant – right now.

The passing of the days are somehow giving weight to the possibilities that he isn't coming back; we truly are over; and that what we had is now ... gone. Why is that? Could it be that past practice has dictated that the men in my life, once they leave, don't come back? Well, not exactly. I mean, sure, there were some who didn't come back; but, there was Blender man who came back better each time; and it ended when I realized that we really weren't good together.

There is also Jacob, who time and again kept coming back and each time we took a few steps forward – until that is, he'd put on the brakes. He's been doing that since the first week I've known him. Each time he did, I would change; I'd grow just a little bit more. Not for him, but because of the opportunity he presented to me.

I've ticked off each day as if it were a day lost, an opportunity that we've missed, something of value that we've thrown away.

But, what if it wasn't lost? What if each day we are apart is just one more day in which we can better ourselves? It is one step closer to becoming that which the Almighty has designed for us to be; on our own, with our own lives, doing what we need to do to become the best of what we can become? What if it is not a day lost, but an opportunity gained to do what we need to do without the interference of the other?

I look back over the last two months and realize all the changes I've made; the way I handle situations; the way I treat people; the signs I'm getting from the Almighty; and the ones that I follow without question. These are all good things – they are steps in the right direction; that being the direction I think the Almighty wants me to go in.

Over the course of the last two weeks I've seen the Almighty' hand in showing me not to accept sex when I want love; to see the manipulative actions of others and how to steer clear of them, and the rewards of doing so; I've reacted differently to a situation with my youngest son that surprised the daylights out of him, and comforted me; I also see the signs that tell me to ... wait. And, I guess, through it all, I realize I am not the same person I was just two months ago; I am better, stronger, more willing to take the time to do something after I've thought it out.

I've a better handle on my financial situation; I'm more comfortable at university; I'm relaxing in my Judaism and Hebrew classes and not putting quite so much pressure on myself for perfection; and I'm learning how to be stable in the face of adversity. I trust more, believe more, and ... well ... I'm not quite so apt to jump through someone else's hoops just because THEY want me to.

Through this alone time I am learning how to take better care of myself; to buy things for me that make my life just a little bit easier or nicer; and to be joyful (hard as it is sometimes) in the things that comprise my life. I'm learning to take this time to do what I need to do ... for me.

Right this minute I'm looking out the patio door at the trees just outside my flat. It's Autumn; so the leaves are turning colors, some are already falling off. But, the wind is blowing and they are being tussled about; their branches going this way and that. For the most part the sun is shining, to be broken by the temporary grayness of the passing clouds. For nearly four years I've sat and looked at those trees; watched them change their look with each passing season; watched them be tussled about by the wind and rains; watched them go from beautiful fall colors, to the bareness of winter, to the buds of spring, and then the lushness of summer. Through it all they still stand; and more importantly, perhaps because of it all they ... grow.

It's been a very difficult year for me; I've seen some really hard times, did some things I wasn't really proud of, made amends where I needed to, and how I could; and it feels like I'm starting ... over ... again. A new season, a new beginning; take the good, leave the bad, and stay away from the ugly.

Yom Kippur was the beginning of a new year for me; this being my worst emotional month of the year was a very good time to start anew. Maybe like the trees, this is again a time to be beautiful, to shed the old and make way for the new, to know there is value in just ... waiting, resting, being still. Perhaps, just perhaps, this will be the first of my best years yet. ☺

SUMMARY

Did you see a parallel to an issue in your own life? The following ten questions may help you gain new perspective on how to manage it.

Questions to ponder:

1. Is this issue bigger than me?

2. What is my part in resolving the issue?

3. Is now the right time?

4. What's stopping me?

5. How do I remove the barriers?

6. What resources will I need to get started?

7. What resources do I have?

Answers to Act on:

8. What isn't working?

9. What is working?

10. What's the next step?

To do List:

Step 6

August

Step 7

Humbly asked Him to remove our shortcomings.

~ *Alcoholics Anonymous*

THE OTHER WOMAN

My once-dearest Jacob,

What am I supposed to say? You came to me on Friday morning, giving me aid, telling me all kinds of wonderful things; weaving all kinds of dreams that we can make come true; then come Sunday night you tell me that your ex-girlfriend is coming to visit and you'll touch base with me when she leaves?

In what language is this supposed to be okay? In what way am I to not be hurt and infuriated by this mockery of "love"? (How would you feel if the tables were turned and it was I inviting my ex-boyfriend to my home and my bed while putting YOU on hold?) How can I not be hurt when you tell me you love me, how very happy I make you, how at home you feel with me – and then you'll be inviting the woman you are "in love" with to share your bed, your home, you? All the things I'd hoped to be mine you give to another and I'm just supposed to accept this and be good with it? I'm supposed to believe your hollow words when your actions are screaming something else?

I can't. I'm not a blind nor stupid enough woman to say, "Oh, that's okay. Go shack up with the one you are in-love with; give her your bed, your home, your life and I'll just be waiting for you when you get around to me." I am deeply hurt and even more angered, believing that you knew of her visit when you told me that I was the only one in your life; I feel betrayed by your deceitful actions of Friday morning as you knew all along you were going to have another this week.

How can I not be devastated when your list of priorities are: you, your work, your children; then your family, your friends, your home; then it's your ex-girlfriend, your poker playing; your drinking ... and then ... sometimes ... when you have absolutely NOTHING better to do ... me. When, if you meant the words you spoke Friday, it should be you and I ... and then everything else. You make concessions for her, but, it's gotten to the point that no matter what I ask of you, the answer is always ... no.

Okay, Jacob. I get it – you have no room for me in your life; you have no want for me; you have your list of priorities set in stone; I refuse to continue being last on that list; I have far too much respect for myself to be so disrespectfully treated by you or anyone! You aren't worth that level of pain, believe me!. You told me that you knew in my heart of hearts I believed you'd always be back. It is these actions that confirm, no, I don't. I never did --- unless and until you change your ways for good, I never will. I am not your best bud; certainly, you wouldn't dream of treating anyone you liked like this. In the back of your mind, you always knew I'd be there for you; I'm not any more, not as a bud, a friend, your business partner, nor the one to share my bed or my life. However; maltreat me again, and you have yourself to thank or to blame for the consequences.

I'm bored and tired of fighting you. I know the truth of who you are, the good, the bad, and the (increasingly) ugly; and I loved you anyway. I thought I needed you in my life; and more importantly, I thought I wanted to be a real part of your life and you a real part of mine. You've shown me that you simply aren't capable of it, as there will always be something or someone more important to you than ... me, than us. Perhaps that is as G-d intended.

I won't be here for you when she leaves, Jacob. I refuse to be yours and "not yours" anymore. Once more, you have yourself and your repulsive behavior to thank or blame for this..

All my words and actions are accomplished with grace, but also with resolve.

C

A GOOD CRY

I don't cry over much.

Though I am sure there are those who would disagree with me.

Sure there's the heart-tugging commercial, the sappy chick flick, the unexpected kind gesture, but other than those things, what's to cry about? Oh, wait; I forgot physical and emotional pain. What was I thinking?

So it came as a surprise to me how some people just make me weep – openly even. Though I don't cry in front of them, I do find myself crying rather often on the phone when they break out in song; when they say they love me to death; and even when they said they don't want to continue the relationship. Yeah, I was a weeping willow; what's your point?

It was through this incredibly brief, but emotional, relationship with Jacob that I remembered something; just how to-the-soul good it feels to cry. The mere act of letting the tears flow drains you of toxins in your system; it empties your cup to make room to fill it up with the good stuff.

Crying reminds me of rain — the way the rain washes the dust from everything; the way the air smells fresh once more; the comforting feeling to know that all is new again. I've always had a fascination with the rain, with thunder and lightening storms. Some may say it relates to the day I was born when it's reported that three tornadoes hit the town where I was born. My grandmother was always quick to add, "No, no. I believe there were four." It may be because on the days my sons were born, it stormed; although one was born in October, the other in April; and both in Michigan. It could also be that it rained a solid downpour for four straight days before my son's wedding, only breaking at noon on his wedding day. When the storms come, and they do come fast and hard, I sit in the living room and watch them; it's a comfort somehow.

I told Jacob about my 100 days of tears. There was a point in my life when I was so downtrodden, that I cried for 100 straight days. After hearing my tail, he agreed that after 30 plus years of sorrow, it just may take that long for all the toxins, to be purged. It was then I realized it was only through the love of family that I stopped the tears and began living my life again.

Life is pretty darn good and a nice hard cry is good for the soul. Please pass the tissue.

KVETCH

My Dearest Jacob,

And so it was brought to my attention, not unkindly – but quietly, that tomorrow is promised to no man or woman for that matter; and today is a gift to be cherished.

This being said, I reflected on our kvetch (which, by the way is a minor stumbling block, a complaint, or a worry) yesterday and I realized something. We were worrying about tomorrow – the possibilities of disappointments, of unmet expectations, of mistakes made, of unfounded fears and worries; when we should have been celebrating our good stuff and working on making our lives better.

Whereas you believe that I am too focused on the future, commitments, and expectations – it is you who are worried about them, and in an effort to make your position of non-commitment crystal clear, I mistook them for a change in our current position of a positive stance, to the negative of you actually breaking up with me. I heard that I was losing one of my dearest friends; and the thought saddened me, hence the tears.

There is no doubt that I enjoy what we have in the bedroom but what you are outside of the bedroom is so much more amazing. I respect and adore you; I find your insights and perspectives to be a welcomed treasure; and I feel that together (in however loosely you want to define this) we are exponentially better than we are separately.

Which brings me to the point of this letter; whereas your stance is one of keeping the possibilities open for tomorrow and worrying about the "What ifs"; mine is to build on today. If we are good today, we will be good tomorrow; if we are not good today, then we need to work on it. I want to spend time with you, see you, talk to you, be with you, NOT because I'm trying to further a relationship or make you commit to something you are not sure of; but because I like you, I enjoy your company, it makes my days more joyful. I don't want to feel like our time together is a commitment you feel obligated to keep, but something that you enjoy, that you see value in, and that you can look forward to as well. I want you to see them as an opportunity to have fun, get to know each other, and a respite from the outside world.

I feel that you just need to relax, quite worrying about what if you disappoint me, what if you don't fall in love with me, what if ... fill in the blank. That's NOT today. Let's worry about the "what ifs" IF and/or WHEN they happen. Cuz, they aren't happening TODAY. Do not be afraid of making tentative plans with me because you may feel (for whatever reason) that they may not come to fruition and hence would disappoint me; cuz, what if it is ME who can't make them happen? For example, what if we HAD planned to get together on Thursday, and Wednesday the kids decided they wanted to go to the zoo instead; would I have had to tell them, "No, we've made plans with Jacob, so we HAVE to go there"? Or couldn't I just have called you and explained the situation and maybe even invited you to come with us? Or what if we had made plans and they actually happened and everyone had a good time? There will always be disappointments in every relationship; the trick is, to not let the minor disappointments overshadow all the positive surprises.

Life changes too fast, there are too many things that are outside of our control to worry about all the "what ifs" which may or may not even happen. We have enough to worry about, adding the element of what if puts too much of a strain on me, and hence, I get emotional and can't think straight, and get confused. And, I think what I should have done was clarified the situation with a "Do we need to make this decision RIGHT NOW?" or maybe even, "What does that have to do with us RIGHT NOW?" If I had realized that you were projecting a what if scenario into the picture, not a today situation, I would have simply derailed the whole situation with a "Let's worry about that if/when the time comes."

You're not the only one who needs to learn how to derail or handle my situations; I need to learn how to calm your fears and settle your worries as well; and I think the only way to do that is to get you back into the NOW – cuz right now, baby, we are at a crossroads – we can be good, or we can let this little pebble destroy everything we have. I'd rather keep us in a good place, one day at a time. How about you?

With grace, and appreciation for all that you are,

C

SUMMARY

Did you see a parallel to an issue in your own life? The following ten questions may help you gain new perspective on how to manage it.

Questions to ponder:

1. Is this issue bigger than me?

2. What is my part in resolving the issue?

3. Is now the right time?

4. What's stopping me?

5. How do I remove the barriers?

6. What resources will I need to get started?

7. What resources do I have?

Answers to Act on:

8. What isn't working?

9. What is working?

10. What's the next step?

To do List:

Step 7

September

Step 8

Made a list of all persons we had harmed, and became willing to make amends to them all.

~ *Alcoholics Anonymous*

TEMPER TANTRUMS

My Dearest Jacob,

I re-read our e-mails from last night and one thing struck me between the eyes; it was only when I became honest with you, that the tables turned and you became incredibly abusive, i.e. screw me and forget me; as that's what I do to you. It was fine for you to tell me just how very "not good enough" I was for you; for you to hide behind the guise of honesty and discount all that I had given you with the false bravado of how you didn't want a relationship; but, when it was me being honest with you -- well -- that became a whole different story. A story, I might add, that we've lived a dozen times, in as many situations.

When it is me helping you, all is right with the world; when it is me allowing you to do as you please when you please, then Jacob is very good. When it is all about Jacob, and Jacob calling the shots, life is grand. But, the minute I ask for something in return, when I make my needs or wants or desires known, well, then I'm just being clingy, or needy, or pushing things. (Which couldn't be further from the truth and you know it!) You've no qualms in taking that which I offer; and equally none when telling me I ask for too much in return; or worse yet, denying me that which you've done and I've mentioned that I enjoy it.

Additionally, you don't hold back when you feel the need to push me away and make me feel that it is all **my** fault; that it is **I** who need to change to become acceptable to you; or it is **I** who needs to make concessions to be with you. Changes, and concessions, and conditions, tempered with just how much you've had to drink, I might add, which change with the situation -- and are ones that you, yourself, are not willing to make or give me.

Your words last night were harsh, and stung, and were said in anger fueled by your fear and your drinking. They also made me realize this morning that the hurt I've felt for the last week was merely nothing more than my injured ... pride; caused part and parcel by your ... fear and drinking.

I don't know who hurt you, but it wasn't me; though it is I (and us by association) that is paying the price -- and it is a heavy price at that. You NOT wanting a relationship is about as much bull as you could possibly throw -- oh, you WANT a relationship, but on YOUR terms; and YOUR terms only. That's not possible in an ADULT relationship.

You were right about not having met your equal before; you are accustom to dealing with little girls (not much more than puppies really) who are more than happy to do as you want for no other reason than to make you happy (jumping through hoops for the tid-bits you give them). You have not been privy to a real ADULT relationship; where give and take are the norm, they are the basic standard for any type of relationship -- including friendship. You are accustom to setting the boundaries for a relationship and expecting (dare I say "demanding") them to be followed; no questions asked, no suggestions allowed, no changes accepted. You, in effect, sir, are a spoiled brat!

Yes, you can be kind, and loving, and funny, and a great guy to bounce ideas off of, a trusted supporter, and wonderful (when you chose) in the bedroom; but, the MOMENT something is required of you, you mount your steed of self-righteous indignation and ride away; claiming unfounded hurts as your foundation to justify your actions. That is no way to have a relationship of any kind; let alone the actions acceptable for an adult man.

As a case in point, when I told you my goals and dreams and aspirations and how I couldn't see you fulfilling them; they were a surprise to you. Why? Because you never bothered to ASK me what mine were. Yes, I know all about yours -- what you dream of, where your haven is, how you feel about your family; what your life goals and objectives are; but, do you know mine? Of course not, because in this relationship, it's all about JACOB -- what JACOB wants, needs, is willing to put up with, is willing to accept. And, quite honestly, it is I who have had enough.

I love you Jacob, I have been in love with you since the moment you broke out in song; I adore you, respect you, cherish you; but, I need a man, not a little boy, an alcoholic, certainly not a spoiled brat. And if there ever comes a time when you want to see all the joys and wonders of a real ADULT relationship; let me know. Cuz this childish, temper tantrum, sticks-and-stones-won't-break-my-bones stuff just doesn't cut it in MY world; a world that welcomes you if/when you are ever ready to reach a bit higher than the bottom of the barrel.

HOPE VS FAITH

Dear G-d, please hear me.

"Hello, G-d. Thank you for all the good stuff you've given me, and the bad stuff that I'm learning from."

I realize, contrary to some popular structured religions, there is no right way to pray. However, I couldn't have been more stunned when I'd asked Jacob how he prayed and he answered with the first response.

The shocking thought that went through my head was, "As if He WOULDN'T?" It was beyond my realm of comprehension to believe that I could pray, and G-d wouldn't hear me. It bothered me for days that my method of prayer as listed in the second sentence would be one of thanks, when another was asking (dare I say, begging?) just to be heard.

I felt his opening sounded as if he were saying, "Please, G-d, if you've nothing better to do, and you've got a few minutes, and I'm so very unworthy, would you please consider, for just a moment, my menial life?" It was as if he were ... hoping ... that the Almighty would give him a moment of His time and in the same breath doubting that He would. (A really scary thought is if Jacob couldn't have faith in the Almighty, what chance did I have that he would have faith in me?)

I don't normally pray in any traditional sense of the word; actually, I've been accused of "talking" not "praying". Maybe it's because there is never any doubt in my mind that G-d hears me, understands me, and is there to help me find the way He has designed for me. The only problem is, I don't always understand what He wants me to do, so I'm in need of guidance when the road is rough or the decisions many. I have faith that He hears me and when I ask for help, He gives it to me.

Perhaps in this matter the differences lay in that Jacob hopes and I have faith; he wonders and I have no doubt; he questions and I obey.

Yet, I can't help but wonder, isn't hope and faith a two-way street? Not so much between hope *and* faith; but between humans and the Almighty? If we HOPE the Almighty hears our prayers, does He HOPE we will listen when He gives us direction? If we have FAITH what we are asking for will be resolved, does He have FAITH we will do as He asks of us? If we KNOW He is there to help us, does He KNOW we will take His help when offered?

What if we stopped hoping and started to have faith? What if we had the courage to believe that not only does G-d hear us, but has faith IN us? What if we stopped hoping G-d will answer our prayers, but had the faith that He's waiting for us to ask for help? What if we stopped asking Him to hear us and just believed that He did?

What if there was NO doubt?

Regardless of our religious beliefs, we all have a few things we can count on: G-d loves us, wants only the best for us, and has faith in us. Could we do no less than to return the favor?

G-d does not have doubt in us; how can we have doubt in Him? Or do *we* just have doubt in *ourselves*? Why is it WE can't believe G-d does love us, is available to us, and He has faith in us? Is it because we feel so very small, so very fragile, so very ... unworthy ... that we can't believe He can see the value in us, that He would have time for us, that He doesn't rejoice in helping us?

Yet, would WE believe this about OUR children? Of course not, we love them unconditionally. Regardless of how many times they disappoint us, no matter how badly they mess up their lives with the decisions they make; we still love them, believe in them, and have faith in them that they will be okay. And we are always there for them to help them as we are able.

So why is it, we have the arrogance to doubt the ultimate Father? Why arrogance? Because how arrogant could we be to believe that WE know what the Almighty believes more than He does? Why is it so very difficult for us to believe that even when WE don't believe in us, He does?

Whether we want to admit it or not, we have to accept that G-d loves us as no one else is capable of loving us. We are his children. As our Father, maybe it is He who hopes we will listen, until such time as He can have faith that we will.

When we hope, we leave open the possibility of doubt; when we have faith, there is no doubt. Perhaps it isn't just a matter of having faith in the Almighty, but needing to live a life so He can have faith in us; and being smart enough that when He gives us a gift, we cherish it; not throw it away. I hope Jacob will listen.

SECRETS

Secrets are a wonderful thing.

If you just so happen to be in the second grade.

It's been some time since I first woke up at Jacob's home. Time is a funny thing; days can past like minutes; seconds can take weeks. It is said to get to know someone, really *know* someone, it takes time. To this I'd like to add, and observation. We can't just spend time with someone; we have to observe them in situations, different situations, and with different people. We have to listen to the way they talk to other people, the words they use, and watch the expression on their faces.

It's easy to explain away things. We'd like to believe what comes out of people's mouth is the truth; usually it is, even though they don't know it.

The first time he suggested I visit his home, Jacob was very excited; he told me several times that his home was in fact, an extension of himself. "If you can accept my home," he said proudly, "then you can accept me."

He wasn't joking. His home was open and spacious; impeccably decorated; complete with candles and the homey touches; meticulously organized with a specific place for everything, and everything in its place; and overall comfortable with style. The walls were painted in varying shades of cool blues and gave the feeling of calm with more live plants than some small greenhouses. He was very sure to tell me it wasn't a designer who decorated his home; but he did; everything from the furniture to the paintings on the wall to the window treatments to the color schemes. I felt very comfortable here; felt it was decorated just the way a woman would want it to be.

So, why is it, do you think, upon wakening in his bed my very first thought of the day was, "Are those Victorian curtains? No man should have patterned Victorian curtains in his bedroom."

But, I let it slide. After all, it wasn't my home; it was his domain. I realize I was letting a lot of things slide; the way he would declare with robust what a "Man's Man" he was; how he'd remind me of how irresistible he was; how he was Mr. IT (as in having that indescribable wonderful 'it' factor). He was ever so concerned with convincing me how manly he was I took it for being a shade too insecure; and let it slide.

Yet, it was another Saturday night when we'd broken another three days of silence and was in the "make up" part of the relationship he said one word that gave me reason to pause. It was simple enough; we were watching the televised karaoke competition; I wasn't facing the screen as I was facing him; when someone came on singing the old bluesy tune, "Stormy Weather" by Ella Fitzgerald. I really liked it and started swaying to the tune thinking just how closely this song mirrored our relationship. Without warning, Jacob yelled out, "Faggot!" I pulled away from him and the look on his face was one of disgust. "That guy is such a FAGGOT!" he exclaimed. It was then I realized the person singing *wasn't* a woman, but was a man who was singing just as well as Ella herself.

I was concerned. Not because he used the term, though I wasn't really keen on it; but because his reaction was such an over-reaction to something that didn't matter at all. Oddly enough, in my travels, I'd never heard a straight man use the term; and had never heard a gay man use it with such venom. To me, this was a term men who were on the fence about their own sexuality used. Doesn't mean it's true, just my experience. In the back of my mind a thought tickled; it was a gentle reminder of all the other times when he'd made slight comments that echoed the same sentiment.

There was just something about the constant insistence of how manly he was that made me think one of two things; either he was unsure of his own sexuality, or, he was a player; a man who would hook a woman and when he was sure he had her let her go and be on to the next conquest. Players generally use women to make themselves feel good; to reaffirm their own manliness; it's a game to them where the more women they have on the line, or go through in the shortest amount of time, the more manly they feel. Who was he trying to prove his manliness to, me or himself?

It wasn't until Monday night the issue really came to a head. When he called late on Sunday night he said he'd call me on Monday to see about getting together on Tuesday. I was good with this – until he didn't call.

Monday night I left him a voice message, knowing full well there was a better than even chance he'd delete it without listening to it. I sent him an e-mail saying the very same thing, basically that

I'm sorry I was out most of the night and missed his call; one I knew he hadn't made. I also innocently stated I'd hoped he and his friend, Brian, had a great day at golf and they couldn't have picked a better day for it.

He exploded! He sent me a scathing e-mail in essence stating I was too high-maintenance for him to handle; to pretend we'd never met; it was over between us; and several other undesirable statements making his position of never wanting to see me again very clear.

I didn't answer his response right away. Yes, I was hurt, but part of me was also relieved. I no longer had to wait for the other shoe to drop; it just did. But, I was also confused. I didn't see where anything I'd asked for was demanding, let alone high-maintenance – I just expected him to do what he said he'd do. I wasn't being unreasonable and had kept the contact to a minimum so as not to be intrusive or pushy. I knew he had destroyed everything we had, or could have had, because he was trying so hard to push me away for no other reason than he was afraid.

I could see his fear; his frustration; his anger in his response. And I didn't know why I was evoking all of these emotions from just a simple statement. Then I realized something; Jacob had a secret. He had told me once when I reveled something intimate about myself that this information was "my secret" and how I should keep *all* of my secrets to myself. I'm not sure what his secret is and I'll not hazard a guess here; but he's fighting too hard to protect it. He is so afraid of anyone finding out what it is, is so terrified of someone getting close enough to him to figure it out, that he is willing to throw away all we could have had just to keep his secret.

Yes, secrets are a great thing; but when you destroy everything good in your life just to protect them; out of fear of someone finding out what they are; then they are not worth having.

I will miss him.

SUMMARY

Did you see a parallel to an issue in your own life? The following ten questions may help you gain new perspective on how to manage it.

Questions to ponder:

1. Is this issue bigger than me?

2. What is my part in resolving the issue?

3. Is now the right time?

4. What's stopping me?

5. How do I remove the barriers?

6. What resources will I need to get started?

7. What resources do I have?

Answers to Act on:

8. What isn't working?

9. What is working?

10. What's the next step?

To do List:

Step 8

October

Step 9

Made direct amends to such people wherever possible, except when to do so would injure them or others.

~ *Alcoholics Anonymous*

NOT TO ME

My Dearest Jacob,

I guess you found someone who needs you - or anyone who can take care of her and get her out of the mud of her life. Be careful though, for as I tried to help you out of your mess, you are trying to help her out of hers, and as you've done to me, she just may leave you for someone ... else; someone more to her social standing. That is, AFTER you've done all the things she needs you to do. I don't know why you feel the need to pay this penance, but you do.

You really hurt me when you kept saying what a "good girl" she is ... like I'm some tart. I guess you never realized that the mark of a true lady is the ability to be a lady in the street and not in bed. Who were you really trying to convince? Me or you?

You never gave me the opportunity to show you that discretion really is the better part of valor. Yet, it wasn't me who asked you to fix my trailer, or shovel my walks, or do my laundry, or put me up for week. What really kills me is you could do all of that for her -- but you couldn't even take me to dinner or go to Wal Mart with me. The drunk and the trailer trash -- a fine couple indeed -- seems you've found your perfect match. When you fall -- you do fall far, I'll give you that.

You tell me you love me, how I'm the only one in your life, and then turn around and say how you've rekindled the flames with one of your high school loves; and that I should be HAPPY for you? How can I?

Again, you dive into a beer can, throw a temper tantrum, and tell me just how much the low-life scum you hang with are better than I am for you; yet, they can do NOTHING for you but drag you down. Oh, wait! That's what you want, isn't it? Someone who you can help -- but can't help you? Someone you can take care of ... but you can't even take care of yourself? Someone who makes you feel proud because you are better than they are -- but, how good are they? How far down that social scale do you have to reach before you find someone lower than you are? Oops. Guess you answered that one with Bunny. Sadly, you couldn't reach across and take my hand.

You were right all along, I expected so much more from you -- I expected you to be the man you are, not the drunk, the liar, the cheat, the .... trailer trash. You didn't get out of that rat hole -- you just changed geography. I saw in you a man of honor, someone respectable, and who liked nice things. I didn't realize you really WOULD let just ANYONE into your home, or into your bed. Why am I surprised that you lied when you said you wouldn't, when you've lied about everything else?? I don't know; I shouldn't be. I guess I should have listened when you said even your daughters wouldn't have anything to do with you; as they know you better. I see why now. (Did they meet Bunny at Thanksgiving?? That would have been wonderful for them!) You ARE a disgrace to them -- by your own choosing -- when you don't have to be.

The bottom line is, I guess you have to ask yourself, if I'm an undesirable for letting you come over at 3 am; what are you for asking and then coming over?? If I'm trash for sleeping with you the first night we met, what are you?? At least I can take comfort in knowing I loved you -- you can take comfort in as you've said all along knowing you just wanted to screw me and forget me. Just remember though -- YOU sought me out; YOU made the moves on me; YOU told me you loved me first; and YOU were the liar. My mistake was in believing you.

Guess it's my turn to screw you and forget you. It won't be that difficult cuz you weren't THAT good. It was all the other stuff that we had that made me love you and fall in love with you.

Sadly, I am grateful for all that we had, but more so, that it is now over. Blessings be to the Almighty. May He be gracious to you and guide you on your journey.

With grace,
your only true friend,
C

MY PART

If I do my part; then G-d will do His.

But, where's the line?

To do my part means that I actually KNOW what my part is. I don't always know what that part is. As an example, I had been sending Jacob e-cards to which he would open yet not respond. The last one he opened said:

My Dearest Jacob,

I was talking to the Almighty this morning, telling him how very grateful I am for all the good things that are going on in my life; how much I appreciate all the lessons I'm learning; how the only piece that is missing is someone to share it all with; and how I wish I could help you through this difficult time of change without feeling like I'm forcing something.

I told Him how I feel that the cards I send you are an intrusion on your life that you neither need them nor want them and that to feel good about me I should really just stop sending them and leave you alone.

He tells me that isn't true; that you really do need to know that there is someone in your corner, someone who has your back, someone who is here for you when you need them ... and someone who loves you anyway.

I guess it was to reinforce His point to me that not only am I writing this, but I'm to send you a message from the both of us ... and the message is:

Lean on me
When you're not strong
And I'll be your friend
I'll help you carry on
Lean on me
For it won't be long
'Till I'm gonna need
Somebody to lean on.
(by Bill Withers)

I need you and the Almighty needs you; we love you, have faith in you; and want you to know we are here for you.

With grace,
and much adoration,
Me and the Almighty

PS We hope this card makes you smile. :)

Although he called me 12 days later, and I did go to see him, he never opened another card that I sent him; so, why bother sending them? He claims to have blocked my e-mail address; so I've not sent him another e-mail either. And although in a moment of weakness I did call him, he didn't answer the phone – so I'll not call him again. I thought I had been doing my part; allowing the Almighty to do His. I guess my part is finished ... at least for now.

Last week at group one of the members asked, "Where is the line between being a good grandparent and being co-dependent?" They had a good point when they illustrated how their grandchild was ill and although the doctor and the parents believed all was well, the member really pushed the issue of getting a chest x-ray. The result was the child had pneumonia.

My Rabbi quoted scripture about a month ago by saying, "It is not our duty to finish the task; however neither are we free to abandon it."

So, again, I ask, "Where's the line?"

At what point do we stop doing and let the Almighty take over? When have we done enough? When have we not done our part and need to do more? When can we say – "okay, I've done my part" and feel good about it?

Ahh, there's the real point, now isn't it? Feeling good about what we've done so we can have the faith that the fruits of our labor will be sweet. But, what if it isn't? What if all the work we've done bears sweet fruit ... for another? I guess it just depends on what we were expecting our actions to do. Were we doing what we were doing for no other reasons than the Almighty told us too? Were our actions dictated by nothing else but the joy of helping another? Or, were we looking for a return on our investment in that we expected to be treated in kind?

If our actions are dictated by the Almighty's' wishes; if they are dictated by the pure joy of helping another, then it really doesn't matter what the outcome is; win, lose, or draw, we can be happy about what we've done. However, if our actions are for the sole purpose of getting a return on our investments, then we are setting ourselves up for a fall. Our actions are no longer pure, they are a method of manipulation; and with manipulation comes the false sense of control. And when that control is proven to be non existent, then we are hurt. We feel betrayed when we've given to another and they don't give back. We become resentful when the gifts we've given to someone they give to another. We are hurt and confused when we don't get the end results we had planned.

But what if we went through life doing for others, and ourselves, as we are able and not expect to get anything in return from the person we are giving to? This doesn't mean that it will hurt any less when the one we love doesn't love us back; but, it does mean that somewhere, someone else will love us in return. It means that what we give out to everyone will be returned; just not necessarily by the one we are giving to. This will give us hope; not so much that we will get back what we give from the person we are giving to – but – that we WILL get it back.

I'd like to be okay with this; but I'm not. I don't know if it is because I am being a willful child or if my sense of justice is offended or maybe it's because I'm not looking at the big picture.

Since I began writing this (about two hours ago) several rather remarkable things have happened. The first was that I realized I'd forgotten my insurance was due and would be cancelled if I couldn't pay the $265 in two days. Not seeing any way to make that happen, I called my insurance agent; who quickly did a "skip payment" to give me a month to come up with it.

I was in the midst of a melt-down over this article when a friend of mine called and asked how I was doing. At first I lied and said I was fine. He got the truth out of me. One thing lead to another and I'll be stopping by his place on my way to work to borrow $35 to get me through until my client check comes in within the week. This will allow me to put $25 in the bank to stop any checks from bouncing; and give me $10 for coffee and smokes.

Then, well, then my oldest son calls me ... just to see how I'm doing and if I'm okay. It was nice that he called to check up on me as the storms have been rather intense as of late.

This all makes me wonder ... could I be right? Could all of the good we give to another come back to us from others? If we don't get what we planned from those we gave to, can we not get it from those who give to us? Is there a balance to the universe? I'm thinking there is.

I'm also thinking that the line between doing our part and letting G-d do his part is at the point where we've actually done all that we can; when we get to the point where we realize there is nothing more we can do in a situation but leave it alone.

I guess we can feel good about what we've done when we've given to another with no expectations of a return and be joyous not only in our actions but in the actions of those who give to us.

Life is not a finite scale of checks and balances; but an infinite opportunity to give and receive.

THE MERRY-GO-ROUND

This is not the first time this situation arose; just one of several.

My Dearest Jacob,

I just walked in the door but a few minutes ago; and received your e-mail message first, so was surprised/concerned to get your two phone messages as well. I have not blocked your number on my cell; however, as there was no other reason, I believe the Almighty once again didn't want me to take your calls. I did call you and got your machine -- I'm nearly certain you were sitting there, screening the call. Why ask/threaten me to call you -- and then not answer? What game are you playing, again, sir?

I don't take kindly to your veiled threats of harm; and am concerned with your propensity to violence. Oddly enough, I heard something today that I thought at the time, and am even more convinced of now, applies to ... us.

It's called the golden gun relationship: It's beautiful, it's shiny, there's some fabulousness about it, it is of great value; but, it's unlocked, it's loaded, and it can blow your head off.

It's part of the cycle of violence: The honeymoon phase: all is right with the world. The buildup stage: things start building up, and we may or may not even know it is happening. Then there is the explosion phase: all Hades breaks loose. Time passes; things calm down. The cycle begins again.

We need space to deal with our own selves first; and then maybe, just maybe, we can try again -- maybe not too; maybe it is better that we are apart then together; and maybe losing each other will be the best thing for each of us. Perhaps knowing that we were too stupid, too lazy, or too afraid to bring out the best -- not the worst -- in the other is a lesson we both need to learn so as not to do it again with the next person we get involved with. Or maybe this is just an unexpected consequence of your drinking.

I've not done anything to harm you or anyone associated with you; I've no idea what you think you have on me to warrant an harassment suite of any kind; though I believe if we were to do a tit-for-tat, your threats would outweigh mine by ten fold; and any action you take against me just may backfire.

As much as I care for you, I no longer chose to have you in my life; not as a friend, a lover, a partner in any venture, or even as someone I would speak to just in passing as you can not be trusted. I will admit there is a part of me that would welcome you to my bed just one more time as it was when you pretended to care about me; but, I'm afraid that it is the friend that I really miss the most. It is the man that I could talk to; laugh with; bounce ideas off of; and whose touch could calm my nerves and soothe my soul who I cry for having lost; as I foolishly believe he was my second best friend in the world.

Feel free to call me to discuss this or any other matter; if I am home, I will answer -- if it is the Almighty's will. May all your blessings be welcome.

With grace,

Cris

PS As to Bob and Mark; Bob is a fake e-mail address, it goes to no one and will bounce if you use it. I use it so that I don't give my friend's e-mail addresses to people they don't know. As to Mark, say what you will; just be cautious that you don't sound like a fool. Remember, Mark has known me for nearly ten years and will see what you say as being 'your truth' not, 'the truth'. He cares very deeply for you; I'd hate to see you ruin that relationship as well.

Oddly enough, the time between your two calls I had this overwhelming urge to again let you ... go. It was at that point that I decided to turn you over to the Almighty one more time; to let him make of us what he will. Sadly enough, I guess I got my answer.

SUMMARY

Did you see a parallel to an issue in your own life? The following ten questions may help you gain new perspective on how to manage it.

Questions to ponder:

1. Is this issue bigger than me?

2. What is my part in resolving the issue?

3. Is now the right time?

4. What's stopping me?

5. How do I remove the barriers?

6. What resources will I need to get started?

7. What resources do I have?

Answers to Act on:

8. What isn't working?

9. What is working?

10. What's the next step?

To do List:

Step 9

November

Step 10

Continued to take personal inventory and when we were wrong promptly admitted it.

~ Alcoholics Anonymous

BIG ... DREAMS

Carrie's Big comes back.

It makes for a nice show.

The reality is, I don't think my Big will come back; and that's something I need to deal with; I just haven't figured out how yet. In the HBO hit series, "Sex in the City", the main character, Carrie Bradshaw (played by Sara Jessica Parker) has an on again, off again, relationship with a guy she refers to as "Big" (played by Chris Noth).

I can relate to her relationship as it mirrored the one I was having with Jacob; complete with the very handsome and equally as unavailable man. However, as much as the television show is set in the glitz and glamour of Hollywood, mine is set in the real world; and the reality is, sometimes they really don't come back; and if they do, they are not worth taking back.

I had a dream; a Big dream, if you will.

Once upon a time, not so long ago, I had a dream; in this dream, Jacob lived with me and I with him; we had his country house and my city flat. His prized possessions melded nicely with mine; and mine his; he had a job he really loved; one that was worthy of him, and gave him what he needed. Jacob had a place safe from the insanity which had become his life; he had a place where he could welcome his children; and he was ... happy.

It was a silly dream; made stronger by the glow on his face when he mentioned in passing the issue of us and marriage; when he told me his secret of it taking a long time for him to accept what I have to offer and implied he had come to accept it; when he told me several times in several ways, he loved me; but it was my dream, and mine alone. This was not a dream I shared with anyone else; nor pictured having with anyone else; it was the dream in my heart, in my soul. Because in this dream there was something else; there was a real relationship between him and I; not the yo-yo that we've always had. We were a part of each other's lives in a real and meaningful way; and as such, I was better than I ever have been; and ever hope to be.

Jacob never understood why all I asked for was to have the good guy; not the drunk guy. Maybe I was wrong for not bearing my real reason for wanting the good guy (the one he only let out enough to show me he was there or to tease me with the possibilities); so, I'll tell you my biggest secret and my biggest fear.

When the good guy is in my life, it is I who is the better for it. When the good guy holds me, touches me, talks to me in his calming voice, makes love to me (not just sex), when he lies beside me in bed, when he makes me feel for however short a time he is with me; that is when I am at my best. I've seen this side of me and I crave it. Sometimes I am almost obsessed with having it because this is the good me which can move mountains; can make magic happen; and can change the world around me. Maybe this is the real reason I love him.

There is a magic when we are good I can't find anywhere else; with anyone else; nor substitute it with anything else; and when it is gone, it is very painful for me. I realize he may not feel this within himself, this fulfillment, this ... joy. For this, I am truly saddened.

Yes, I had a dream; a silly dream; sadly, it is a dream, which may have no hope of actually becoming reality. But still, I pray someday it will.

SPICY

There's oatmeal and then there's chili peppers.

Which kind of man are you looking for?

Personally, I like mine HOT. But there is a price to pay for this spicy kind of life; a price some say is too high and not worth the trouble. I'm not sure if it is yet or not.

About six months ago a girlfriend of mine summarized Jacob as being a chili pepper man; hot, spicy, and best tolerated in small doses. She was right. She compared the men in her life to oatmeal; a ready staple, good for sustenance, but bland. Yes, the men in her life would call when they said they would; made dates for future plans; and actually showed up for the dates they made. All the things chili pepper men don't do as that would reduce the excitement of the unexpected.

I was talking to yet another friend of mine (I only have three, so don't think I just talk to anyone about him) and was telling her how at least she and her guy had something real, they talked every day, got together on the weekend and had something close to what I would deem a normal relationship.

"Yeah," she agreed, "but, I don't have singing, and dancing, and smiling until your face hurts until dawn."

No, she didn't.

To top off all of this, I recalled an e-mail I received a couple of weeks ago which stated that the removal of old securities opens the way to new opportunities. I used to find great security in that when a man said he would call, he did. It made me feel he was living up to his word.

So, what does it mean when Jacob says he will call and doesn't? Does this mean he is not a man of his word? Does it mean he doesn't care about me? Or does it simply mean that for whatever reason which has nothing to do with him or me ... he just didn't pick up the phone.

On the flip side, what does it mean when he does call? It means, he wants to see me. It would be easy to say the only reason he's calling is for sex; but it isn't. I fulfill a need in him that neither of us chooses to put a label on. We laugh, we sing, we dance until dawn; we have stimulating conversation over coffee the next morning, we have passionate sex, and we look about us at the beauty surrounding us and are grateful for it. I will admit, he takes my breath away with his touch and sometimes this scares him. Yet, it's better than the flip side of his touch leaving me cold.

Is it perfect between us? Not by a long shot; but it is hot and spicy and … best tolerated in small doses. It is the spice of my life, not the core nor the sustenance. And for all of the longing, and wanting more, and knowledge that he will never be oatmeal … it is worth it. I know my old securities don't work for him, so I need to set some new ones. I can be secure in several things; that when he does call he wants to see me; that we do have something we can't get from someone else; and that when we get together for just a little while all is right in our worlds.

Until it isn't.

MESSES

My life is a mess.

It's just not as bad as it used to be.

I guess that's where the blessings lie; in the messes, the little messes, and the issues that are no longer as big of messes as they were. But, I don't know for sure.

As I look about me, my flat is clean, dishes done and put away, ditto for the laundry; my studies are caught up; my papers are graded and recorded for the week, I've been keeping up on my Judaism classes okay, I've a couple of packs of cigarettes, some cat food, nearly a full take of gas; but, no rent, no car payment, and no money for the remaining utility bills.

Oh, did I mention, no Jacob either? Perhaps I missed that part. As I've not heard from him in three weeks, I don't know what to think; the Almighty hints that he'll be back in time, just not when and that if logic holds we'll be better than we've been before. I hope that's true.

So, about these messes, what do I do? Well, I could sit and worry and fret and cry; or, I could say, "Oh, well, the Almighty is working as well as He can" and have faith that it will all work out. I mean, I'm doing the best I can with what I have; I just don't know if it's good enough. I think it is, but, I don't KNOW.

I guess that's the problem with messes; you can see them but you just don't know what to do about them. Funny thing is, no one else knows what to do either. There's no one I can turn to for help, or advice, or guidance; cuz they are my messes. So, I'm guessing the only thing I can do is turn them all over to the Almighty and say – it's up to You; I've done all that I can, now it's Your turn. And that's where the leap of faith comes in.

The question now is, can I make that leap? I guess the answer would be: I don't have any other choice.

NO

Sometimes G-d says no.

But, not right away.

The signs from the Almighty are hard to read sometimes; we see something we want, we think He says yes; but then we don't get it; so we think we misread the sign. What we didn't know, was the answer was, "Yes, for now."

"Yes, for now," is like saying "No, for later." We have this habit of believing that what ever is happing RIGHT NOW is what is going to continue to happen until we change something and stop it from continuing to happen.

But life doesn't work that way. If it did, all the good things would continue to be good and all the bad things would continue to be bad. We could never change the bad things to be good things; and, well, we wouldn't change the good things to be bad things. In life, we want the bad things to change to the good things; we just aren't all that pleased when it works the other way around.

Such as it was with Jacob; we were in a good place, nothing has changed us from being in that good place; so why is it a bad place now? Because regardless of how hot the flames, if you don't tend the fire, it will soon become nothing more than ashes.

Three weeks of no contact has reduced us to this on my side of the fence.

I had truly thought that Jacob and I were the real deal; we had all the makings of a long term relationship; and through the last six months or so, I've grown a great deal as a person. So I thought it was the Almighty's way of saying "Yes." However, it has turned into a matter of, "Yes, for now," and the now is over.

Seems this last week has been filled with men who are a "Yes, for now"; though the "now" part has been a matter of a few hours.

First on that list was Temple Joe; needless to say, I met him at Temple. It was simply a matter of asking the Almighty for what I wanted, and Temple Joe walking in the door. He confirmed that the Almighty really does have a wonderful sense of humor in that Temple Joe comprised nearly everything I didn't want in a man, but fit the bill perfectly for a good Jewish Mother if I were so inclined to need one.

Then came Construction Harry; yep, big, burly, smart, sensitive, an overall nice handsome guy. And the only thing I could think of as we sat for a late evening coffee was: He's NOT MY Jacob. He did all the right things, said all the right words; but was NOT who I wanted to be with. He did confirm for me that I'm pretty, smart, sexy, and well worth his time and effort. He, however, was not worth mine as he wasn't who I wanted.

Then came Motorcycle Man; or maybe I should say, came back. He was the one months ago, who took me on the cycle ride and I found my balance. He does that to me, helps me find my balance that is. It was a moment of weakness on both our parts; I was reeling from telling Jacob goodbye (or maybe I should clarify this by saying telling his answering machine goodbye); and he was dealing with a psycho ex-wife and her drama. It ended with us grabbing a bottle of wine, a hot tub, a quick dinner, and conversation until the wee hours of the morning. Although he slept on the sofa-bed, I still couldn't bring myself to sleep in my bed – the one I'd shared only with Jacob.

It was strange being with him after all these months; and as we were getting along so well, I broached the subject as to why it didn't work out with us the first time. With a preference of his comments being how he didn't want to offend me, he simply said, "You've changed." I didn't see any changes, so encouraged him to explain.

And the dam broke!

He let me have it with both barrels; how now I seemed calmer, more confident, less controlling, and less manipulative; and how much he liked this change. He said how he sensed it within minutes of his arrival that he could suddenly say anything and not be afraid of me going off the deep end or judging him if I didn't agree with what he was saying.

I didn't mention that it was only through my relationship with Jacob that I had learned these new skills. I didn't think it important to tell him then, and saw no reason to tell him later.

The Almighty wanted me to see the changes I've made, so sent me someone who could see them. Of course, He also made sure I knew that this guy was NOT MY Jacob either; he was way too much of a slob, took way too many medications, and was no where near as handsome as Jacob is.

The really odd thing is, through them all, my cat hated each of them and made her displeasure known. Upon their arrival she'd run to the door, only to be disappointed as Jacob wasn't standing there. I know how she felt.

So, what do I do now? Well, for today, it's chat with friends; then collect the trash, do the dishes and laundry, Hoover the flat; do some writing; grade papers, work on my own homework assignments, and then have dinner with a girlfriend. Tomorrow, well, the morning is for Hebrew lessons; and the afternoon is still open.

I sit and watch for His signs as to the direction my life is to take; I try to turn all things over to Him; sometimes with claw marks, sometimes without; and I listen, I listen very hard for Him to say, "Yes, for keeps." I do so hope He says soon.

SUMMARY

Did you see a parallel to an issue in your own life? The following ten questions may help you gain new perspective on how to manage it.

Questions to ponder:

1. Is this issue bigger than me?

2. What is my part in resolving the issue?

3. Is now the right time?

4. What's stopping me?

5. How do I remove the barriers?

6. What resources will I need to get started?

7. What resources do I have?

Answers to Act on:

8. What isn't working?

9. What is working?

10. What's the next step?

To do List:

Step 10

December

Step 11

Sought through prayer and meditation to improve our conscious contact with God, *as we understood Him*, praying only for knowledge of His will for us and the power to carry that out.

~ *Alcoholics Anonymous*

GOING BACK

Relationships are not like goulash.

They are not better the second time around; they are just stale.

Like some invisible beacon when I finally shut the door on the relationship between Jacob and I, past loves and lovers knew it and they began their campaign to get me back. It was strange that they would pick now as a time to contact me, as I'd told no one about the breakup and the last they knew I was involved with someone else.

There is no doubt that Jacob had that "WOW" factor; he came in, swept me off my feet, shattered all of my barriers, ran my heart and soul through a meat grinder then walked away just as easily as he walked in.

There is also no doubt that I want to go back; back to a time when I had my balance, my strength, my joy and my life in order. I'm getting there by taking baby steps every day; the joy is a bit harder to capture, but, it's coming back as well.

So, why is it, do you think, that the men who I walked away from are now vying for a second chance? More importantly, should I give them one? If it didn't work out the first time around, what makes me think it will the second time? Hmmm.

Change.

I've changed; they've changed; time has changed all that we had between us. Sometimes that's a good thing; sometimes, as in the case of Jacob, that's not such a good thing. So, why is it that I think if Jacob did come back that we could work it out this time? I don't know; but I think it's not true; I believe I'm just kidding myself.

As with all the others who have walked through my life, there are some things that you just can't go back and recapture; some bridges you can't rebuild, and some loves that are just ... lost.

Sometimes we really do only get just one chance, one chance to make it work, one chance to take it as far as we can, and one chance to be the best we can be.

As I sit and look at my life, compare it to my life of a year ago, think of all the people who've I met, and loved, and yes, even lost, I realize there are some things that are worth going back for … and some things that are best left lost.

May I live so I don't have to go back.

FALLING

I know I fell hard.

But was it necessary for me to watch the man I love fall too?

Sometimes in life we need to learn the lessons by doing; other times we are lucky enough to learn by watching someone else. So, what does it mean if first I had to do the lesson, then I had to watch it?

It seems I entered Jacob's life when he was on the downward spiral. I offered my help, and was chastised for doing so. I offered my support and was tossed away, unwanted, unneeded. I offered my love and was hated for doing so.

The pain in watching him fall and feeling the subsequent rejection because of it is, at times, more than I think I can bear. When Jacob left, and came back, and left again so many times I took him back, ever hopeful that he had changed his ways and really did want the life we could make together. I was mistaken and have paid the price of that hope through more dashed dreams, lies, betrayal, and mental anguish.

Each time Jacob left, I was devastated. I could see the solutions to his problems; offered help and guidance; but his pride would allow him to have none of it. He was determined of two things; the first being he got himself into that mess and he was going to get himself out of it; and proving that even if something was meant to be he could screw it up and lose it.

He did both very well as the bank now owns his house, he lost his business, and I am not a part of his life.

As I sit here on this rainy Monday morning, knowing I need to get ready to go to a job that I love, that pays the bills nicely, and offers me the freedom I need to do other things, I feel a bit ... confused. I live in a nice place, decorated to my high standards, drive a nice car, am attending various classes, and have found a place where I can worship in a manner that suits me. I was willing to share this life; be a part of his; and willing to work to make a good life with him. But, I hurt; deep down inside I hurt so very much for him, for his situation, for his choices which have caused him to lose all that he held dear.

I'm not sure what the lesson is I'm supposed to be learning from all of this. Maybe it is that I have no control over what others do; that I neither caused his plight, nor can cure it. Maybe it is that each of us makes our own choices and is responsible for them and I am neither responsible for his choices nor responsible for the outcomes. Or maybe, just maybe, it is that I should be grateful that he didn't pull me down with him.

Jacob was the second man I'd ever loved unconditionally; I can still say, "I loved you unconditionally; and even though you've left me, I will still be here for you. I still love you."

Perhaps, just perhaps, as the Phoenix rises from the ashes when it is our time, Jacob and I will rise again – to new heights, to new levels that neither of us could have ever dreamed of reaching. Ah, therein lies the prayer … and the hope.

SEASONAL RELATIONSHIPS

I took down my holiday decorations today.

I didn't cry either.

The holiday seasons are strange for me; they are filled with hopes and dreams and prayers for miracles; and justly so, fraught with disappointments. Wrapped in with all the woulda, shoulda, coulda's is the reality of what … is.

We can hope and pray and dream all we want; but there comes a time when for all the good work, and good intentions, and goodness we've put out there, we have to take them back as they are not wanted by another.

So it was I was taking down my holiday tree, one bulb at a time, when I realized just how much like this tree Jacob was. I took a good deal of time adorning him with my goodness; was ever wary that I didn't overdo one side and put things out of balance, and when I had finished my adornments, was pleased just to gaze in wonderment at what had become.

I gave Jacob everything I had and just like the tree, he accepted them, he relished in just how much better they made him; and he gave back … nothing. I was content to just be in the same room with him, such was his addition to my life. Yet even that was asking too much.

It pains me to dismantle my tree; to put all the shiny ornaments away; to wrap up all the lights. But, as I do so, I lovingly recall all the memories certain ornaments represent; and I smile for times gone by.

I know that I'll finish packing them in boxes, put the boxes in the dinning room out of the way, and then I'll load them into my car the next time I go to my son's house and put them in storage. I also know that come next Thanksgiving weekend, I'll take them out of storage and put them back up.

It took me three days to put up my decorations and three hours to put them all away. Perhaps dismantling my emotions for Jacob can happen the same way.

In this hope, I will very gently delete his numbers from all of my phones, take his name off of my e-mail lists, take his photo off of my cell phone, out of my wallet and off my sun visor, and lastly take all the e-mails he sent me and put them in a file and tuck them away somewhere out of sight. Additionally, I know I can't play poker on the site he did, need to find a different route to my son's house so I don't go past his exit, and toss away the sweatshirt and all the other mementos I've kept of his. I'll not listen to the songs which remind me of him, nor go to the coffee shop where we first met.

And maybe, just maybe, if I do all of this the hope of another coming into my life, one who is willing to share and celebrate what we can build together will return.

Maybe just like the hope that returns each December, the hope for new beginnings which come in January will replace it and I can finally be ... whole again.

DAWN

It'd been wishing for snow for some time now.

I got my wish last night.

I wanted the newness of the snow, the hope of a green spring, and ... the quiet. Come to think of it, I got quite a few wishes last night. I'd wished Jacob would call; that we'd get together; that I'd once again wake up with him; and that we could be good again. We did all but the last one.

I'm sitting on the counter again in his robe, again drinking the chocolate coffee black, and again he sleeps in the other room.

It's hard for me to sit here this morning and see the reminders of another's presence. Her cream and sugar sit neatly on the countertop. The food and water for her cat sits on the floor. And mine? Well, my sugar and cream have been tossed away and my cat's treats are no where to be found. I can't help but feel like I'm intruding. It seems odd to no longer feel at home in a place that I've missed for so long.

Never in my fondest dreams could I have orchestrated last night's happenings which lead me here. I'd gone to my 12-step meeting remembering what the Almighty told me that morning; "Be open to the good things that come your way."

So, when after the meeting my friend invited me to dinner, I told her I was broke so she offered to buy, I said yes. When after dinner she threw a $20 at me. I said thank you.

But I didn't hear the phone ring, none of the three times when Jacob called; yet woke with a start as he was leaving a message. Although I wasn't too keen on the message he left me, I did accept his invitation to come over when he extended it.

I see the Almighty' hand every step of the way and I know I am where I belong. I told the Almighty yesterday that I couldn't see a way for us to work out.

I'd convinced myself that if/when Jacob called again I'd go through the options I had and how none of them ended well.

The first option was he came over when he called; late at night was not acceptable. The second was we'd make plans to get together and he'd not show up. The third was I'd just say no.

The idea of me going to him never crossed my mind. Yet that was the invitation; that was why I suddenly had $20 to put towards the gas to get here and that's why the trip was done without a moment's hesitation. Without question when he offered I got up, dressed, packed and left.

The question now is, why am I here? The easy answer is because the Almighty said so. Perhaps a better question would be what do I do now that I am here? The first answer would be – enjoy it. They tell me it's always darkest just before the dawn. Many times I've felt that the separation from Jacob was the darkness.

He said a lot of things last night, some while he was drunk, and others while he was asleep. And although the Almighty told me to ask Jacob what my name was when he talked in his sleep, I didn't have the courage to do so. I was afraid the name he'd say wouldn't be … mine.

I don't know if this is the dawn of a new day with us or not; all I do know is that I listened and this was the answer to my prayers. I could not have possibly known it would be the last time I would see him.

Perhaps that is the true test of a dawn; we never know which one is our last one, so we need to just enjoy each sunrise as they happen.

SUMMARY

Did you see a parallel to an issue in your own life? The following ten questions may help you gain new perspective on how to manage it.

Questions to ponder:

1. Is this issue bigger than me?

2. What is my part in resolving the issue?

3. Is now the right time?

4. What's stopping me?

5. How do I remove the barriers?

6. What resources will I need to get started?

7. What resources do I have?

Answers to Act on:

8. What isn't working?

9. What is working?

10. What's the next step?

To do List:

Step 11

January

Step 12

Having had a spiritual awakening as the result of these Steps, we tried to carry this message to alcoholics, and to practice these principles in all our affairs.

~ *Alcoholics Anonymous*

ON SECOND THOUGHT ...

Jacob,

I've listened to your rantings, your threats, and your accusations long enough. You are not my father, my husband, nor my G-d; you do NOT have the right to try to control me and that is exactly what you've been trying to do since day one. It's always been about what Jacob wants, needs, desires; what YOU can put up with, tolerate, or accept. It's always been Jacob leading the parade, Cris following, Jacob getting scared ... then running away; and Cris suffering the mental abuse because of it. I've done NOTHING to deserve this from you.

Well, guess what? No body really cares what you want. No body cares that you're again riding the horse of false self-righteous indignation. No body cares that you are so afraid of losing the best thing that ever happened to you that you push her away with threats, accusations, and innuendoes. And no body cares that your pride was bruised by a woman who is not JUST your equal, but, quite frankly, your superior.

If you feel you must show your manliness by pursuing your legal options; be my guest. For even IF I did all the things you THINK/KNOW I did it still isn't illegal; the worst that could happen would be I'd be proven a liar; there would be no fine, no jail time, no real judge (after seeing all the facts) who would rule against me. Why? Because YOU kept opening the door -- your own correspondence shows it: "Never contact me again" -- countered within 45 minutes with, "I'll give you tonight to contact me, or ... (implied) else."

Any one who wasn't related to you, or who wasn't trying to do you a favor, once they saw all that you have sent me, would dismiss the situation with a warning -- to both of us; stay clear of the other.

You pushed me past the point of breaking just to see if you could trust me when I said I wouldn't give up on you; to see if I believed you when you said things would be better. I won't give up on you -- I believed you and think things will get better -- I gave you my word and though you may scoff at that, my word is as good as gold. On my honor, I will always believe in you, have faith in you, stand by you, and love you. No matter what you do or say; no matter how hard you try to push me away; no matter how drunk you may get; and no matter what you say to the contrary. To do otherwise would be beneath me. I will not, however, tolerate your abuse any longer. If you want to come at me with guns a blazing, that is your right. If you want to come at me with loving arms, that is also your choice. Just know that I don't back down, I don't give in, and I don't give up.

I am here for you. And, yes, it does sadden me to know what we could do if we were on the same side -- not fighting each other. There is a gift here that we are wasting through foolish pride; both of ours. I can't help but believe that the Almighty never wanted it to get to this.

As always,
with grace,
C

SOMETIMES

Sometimes we go through life, never knowing if we've made a difference.

There's no doubt Jacob made a difference in my life.

I just wish I could say it was a good one; as, right this minute, I'm not so sure. He walked into my life; ripped down all the barriers; made all the bad things go away ... and then became the bad thing.

He left my life as easily as he entered it; hung up the phone, walked away, and didn't look back. He didn't take my calls nor return them; although there were only two. He didn't answer my emails, nor open the cards I sent, although there were few. He made no attempt to contact me, and didn't respond when I contacted him.

He left without so much as a good bye.

And perhaps, just perhaps that was the way G-d had intended all along.

Jacob's main focus was on proving that even if something was meant to be, you could still throw it away; and he did. With no regard for my feelings or emotions or respect to me; he threw away ... us. I know I didn't break him, I can't fix him, and it's not my responsibility to do so. Equally as so, I know I didn't break us, I can't fix us, and again, it's not my responsibility to do so.

All I do know is this, there has yet to be a day when I don't think of him and rarely do those thoughts exclude inducing my tears. I will admit that what once was hours of soul-wrenching sobs has become few minutes of bittersweet tears. The prayer is that at some point the tears will stop; the miracle will be when the thoughts stop as well. I had thought today was going to be that day; I was mistaken.

But perhaps, tomorrow will be the day.

There is a part of me that really envies him with his ability to discard me so very easily; to take such comfort in knowing that he won, that he really did throw away something that was meant to be. It's sad to throw away a gift from the Almighty; sadder still when you ARE that gift that's been thrown away. It hurts to know you meant so very little to another when they meant everything to you.

There was a time when I would have lain down my life for him and he wouldn't even pick up the phone for me. I gave him my heart, my soul, my body, my mind, and all of the gifts I had; he gave me … only what he chose to when he chose.

And maybe therein lies the real lesson; to never love someone that much; to never give that much of yourself; and to never love someone unconditionally who has no use for you in their life.

He left me, and I let him; and therein lay my only comfort. I didn't stoop to begging or pleading; bombarding him with emails or phone calls; I quit fighting him and I lost … but, there was no way to win. I can't make someone love me, or need me, or want me in their life. All I can do is show them what I have to offer and let them decide.

He decided no. He looked at me, at us, and said, "No, thank you; I'll try my luck somewhere else." Well, that's what his actions tell me as he didn't actually SAY anything.

And there is nothing I could have done to change that. All I can do is hope, and pray, that the hurt will one day be gone … as he is.

I hope that day is … soon.

For the first six months after he left, I begged G-d that he would come back; the second six months I begged that he wouldn't; and since then, I've just begged G-d that I would be good either way. It's been over two years since he left.

I'd like to say that I am good; but, I'd be lying.

I don't talk about him to my friends anymore; rarely does his name enter a conversation; but that doesn't mean I don't think of him … it just means that I'm not feeling the need to alienate my friends through talking about him.

I find I don't sleep in my bed anymore; I try, but it's too hard without him there and I end up in the parlor bed before the night is through.

I try not to think about him when I empty the trash, turn off the fan in the living room, do the grocery shopping or the laundry; but I still do. I thought I was doing very well this morning with not thinking about him; that is, until I went to give my cat her meds and for the very first time saw the clothespin he used to close the chip bag.

I lost the calendar sheet that sat on my desk for so long that I got from his desk the first night I stayed there, the one that marked the day we met. I think his sweatshirt is still in the top of my closet. I don't sleep with it anymore but haven't found the courage to throw it away. I still have one of the cigarettes he gave me to tide me over until I picked myself up some; with, I must admit, money he gave me.

I thought we had something real; I could see G-d's hand in it every step of the way. He saw nothing but the bottom of a beer can. Which is why I'm still hurting. If I could see all the good we had; was I blind or fooling myself or just wishful thinking?

Again, I don't know.

I wish I did. I wish I knew, REALLY KNEW that we were over or that he was coming back, or that we would get a second chance. But, I don't. All I know is right this minute he is not a part of my life and I am not a part of his.

I read something a while ago that said: for something to become something great it must first become nothing. Well we are nothing … and maybe we will become something great and maybe we will remain nothing.

And so it was that I'd no more than finished that last sentence, thinking that was where I would end, when a very good friend of mine stopped by. She thought I looked as though I was about to cry; and I told her I'd just been crying.

We sat and we chatted, and I told her about this; and why the tears. She looked at me and said, not unkindly, "Do you want him or need him?"

Without thinking I said, "Need."

"You think??" she asked.

"Yes," I replied and tried, and failed to hold the tears at bay.

"Sooo," she said, "you need him to pay your rent?"

I was shocked at the absurdity of her question, "Of course not!"

"Then you need him to pay the utilities?"

"No!"

"Okay, okay," she said smiling. "You need him to pay for or fix your car?"

"No." I watched my friend sitting there smiling at me as she fired off her questions; and I had no clue to where she was heading.

"Soooo, you need him to clean the house? Do the grocery shopping? How about doing the laundry? Shoveling the snow from your walk? Or putting together your budget?"

At each question, I gave a resounding no.

"In other words," she said very quietly, "you didn't NEED him at all; you just really, really wanted him."

I just stared at her, understanding dawning slowly.

"Do you understand," she said steepling her fingers, "that you are already whole? That you can take very good care of yourself and that you don't NEED anyone to take care of you?"

I didn't know that; I didn't realize that I've been taking care of myself for a long time; but, because somewhere along the line I felt that I SHOULD need a man to take care of me, and because I didn't have one, that I was somehow ... lacking. And therein lay the cause of the real pain; the real agony. I was not whole in my mind, because HE wasn't with me. I just had never really realized that I didn't NEED him to be whole.

Yes, he did make a difference in my life; when he was with me, AND just as importantly, when he left. I would like to believe that I could have learned this lesson on my own; but, I'd be lying to myself. I know that I can't make this journey though life alone; I need G-d, and my family, and my very good friends.

Jacob came into my life, ripped down all my barriers, made all the bad things go away; and when he left, he taught me the most important lesson ... I am very good alone; and more importantly, I don't NEED anyone in my life. I do, however, want someone. And when I am ready, really ready, G-d will provide for that as He does every other aspect of my life.

G-d's will be done ... and may I be good with whatever it turns out to be.

MY DEAR FRIENDS

And so it was that I could take the silence no longer, and called Jacob; of course, for whatever reason, he didn't answer the phone. I left him a message: "No calls, no return calls, and no response to ANYTHING I've sent you. I guess you got what you wanted. Know that I loved you. Goodbye." I wasn't angry, I was ... saddened. I had just closed the door on a relationship that I truly cherished.

I know that many of you said to have patience; just to wait it out and he would come around and realize just how good we had it, would want it, and would reach out and take it. When? When was he going to do this?? Well, I did wait; three weeks I waited for a phone call, an e-mail, a smoke signal even, something -- ANYTHING -- and nothing came. And every day I would go about making my life happen, every day I resisted the temptations to succumb to underhanded tricks, or sending a barrage of messages; I am proud of my actions in this regard. But, every day I would still cry because I missed him so very much; and every day I would worry that something had happened to him; and every single day I would pray that Jacob would accept the gift G-d had given him ... me. But, he didn't. He didn't call, or write, or accept the gift -- he gave it back. There is nothing short of him being in a coma that could excuse this blatant disregard of me for so very long; and the fact is, it was a silent good bye that was a long time coming. He's said from the beginning he did not want a relationship; and although his previous actions said contrary, the bottom line is, he got what he wanted.

With his actions, or lack thereof, he told me, and he told G-d, that he didn't want me. So be it. I did want the gift G-d had given me; I did want Jacob; but, he's not mine to keep. It's sort of like getting that shiny new bike that you wanted for your birthday; but, the pedals are broken so you have to take it back and you realize that the store doesn't have another one and they can't get the parts to fix it. You want the bike, but it's broken; and although you loved it, broken and all, ya still can't ride it.

I've made a lot of changes in my life over the course of the last few months; Jacob was a big part of those changes. I learned how to listen more closely, judge less harshly, accept more willingly, to wait longer, to love more, to trust without conditions, to laugh at every opportunity, to do what I need to do to make my life happen no matter what anyone else is doing, to accept the gifts and opportunities G-d affords me, to have faith, and ... when to walk away.

I will miss him dearly. I still believe if G-d wants it to happen it will; but, I also realize that sometimes we turn our heads away and don't accept the gifts He has given us. Unfortunately, we are not the only ones hurt when we do this; we hurt the other person too.

Know that I love you all, appreciate your friendship, but, I may not respond as quickly as I normally do; the darkness is so very dark it's hard to see the light right now. This too, shall pass.

L'Shana Tova!
(To a good year)

With grace,
Cris

LIVING SIMPLY

I woke up alone this morning.

And I smiled.

There is something to be said for waking up with the right person beside you; there is also a great deal to be said for waking up alone ... and being content with it. There is a certain comfort to getting back to the routine (as my mother would say); get up, feed/water the cat, start the coffee brewing, check the emails, have the first smoke of the day, write, talk to the Almighty, plan your activities ... and just breathe.

Today is not a remarkable day; it is a normal day filled with work, school, miracles, pleasant surprises, comforts, and well ... I guess it really IS a remarkable day; for what isn't in it.

The fear of not having groceries, or gas in the car, or making the bill payments; the anger of others not treating me the way I feel I deserve to be treated; the distrust of those in my inner circle; the anxiety of not knowing what is going to happen next; and the overwhelming pain of not being where I need to be ... are all missing from my life.

They have been replaced by the trust in the Almighty to show me where He wants me to be, the comfort of knowing I'm finally in a healthy relationship with myself and my friends, the belief that I am doing just what I'm supposed to be doing, and the ... excitement ... of seeing all the things I've yet to do and the confidence of knowing I can do them ... in time.

Waking up alone adds balance to my life; it no longer holds the fear that I will always be alone; it offers me the opportunity to do what I need to do, when I need to do it, to get to where I need to be. It affords me the space I need to be good alone, with the comfort of knowing I'm never alone – the Almighty is always with me, He does hear my cries, my laughter, my inner dreams, and my joy.

He sends me those who can teach me and learn from me. I don't have to keep looking for teachers. I can relax and know He will send them to me. As with all things there is a certain balance: learn/teach; give/receive; with another/alone. The trick is being balanced in the first place, so you can swing from one to the other; and that is the best place to be in. ☺

IT'S NOT WORKING

I've found the perfect mate.

So, why can't I love him back?

They tell me that each relationship changes the next one you have. I think they are right; that doesn't mean it's a good thing.

I've been "seeing" this man since two days after I learned Jacob claimed he was engaged. I caved in only in an attempt to "get over" Jacob – it's not working. What is working, however, are the lessons Jacob taught me; those, yes, those are working very well. I can see why he used them as there is a nice comfort level to knowing someone is at your beck and call, permanently at arm's length, and not caring about them in the slightest.

I would tell you this new man's name, but I don't use it ... ever. He thinks me calling him "Sweets" or "Dear" or "Love" is endearing, that I'm building a close, personal relationship. What he doesn't realize is that half the time I can't remember his name, and the other half, well I chose not to use it. Calling someone by their name is ... personal; and that just isn't in the lessons Jacob taught me.

I've met his kids, his parents, and his close friends. I like them well enough. I actually like his ex-wife; we could almost become friends. We had barbeques in the fall, went on a couple of hay rides, and I even attended his Temple on more than one occasion. He, however, did not go with me to visit my mom at Halloween, nor over the Christmas holidays, and certainly didn't go with me when I went to visit my son and his children over New Year's weekend. To think of talking about my friends and family members to him is just too far outside my comfort zone as is he coming to MY Temple.

His friends and family think we are the perfect couple. Again, I say his as my friends don't know anything about him; not his name, not his occupation, nor that I'm even seeing anyone. That was another of those lessons I've learned – if no one knows about him, then they can't give me advice, tell me I'm wrong, or make comparisons. If he is hidden in my life, my dirty little secret, then when I break it off with him, no one can call me a fool.

I don't go to his house in the middle of the night, and he certainly doesn't stay the night at mine. His house is not my … home; and I don't respect it as such. We don't dance and sing off-key till dawn, laugh until our faces hurt, or make love to the point of seeing stars. We don't know what the other is thinking by the look on their faces, hold each other when we cry, or tell each other our secrets. I have yet to let him kiss me, let alone share my bed. He's quick to open my doors, take my arm when we're walking, and help me with my coat. His manners are sterling and I appreciate them.

Fact is I appreciate a great deal about him. He's smart, degreed as I am. He's a professional, well respected in his field, socially acceptable, and smoking hot handsome. He knows his wine, his geography, and where to buy the best chocolates. We attend the theatre, black-tie gatherings, benefits for social causes, and just as easily stop by McD's on the back of his motorcycle, and make it an impromptu picnic at a local park.

We spent New Year's Eve at the Ritz and I would highly recommend it; yet, he knew I would not kiss him when the bells tolled twelve. Just as he knew equally as well that the room he rented for the night would have two beds and he would sleep alone. Yet, he would rather face a firing squad then cheat on me; he doesn't even look and I know, as I've watched the way other women put the moves on him and how he blindly disregards them as a gentleman should.

I haven't figured out why he wastes his time when he knows that we are going no where; I've made it very clear that I don't want a relationship with him; yep, just like Jacob did to me. There is nothing he can say or do to change my mind as there was nothing I could do. But, now I do know what it's like to have someone be head-over-heels in love with you; and you not give a rat's ass about them. I now fill Jacob's shoes rather nicely and understand completely, regardless of how foreign and empty it is to me. It's easier to be empty, filled with longing for another, than to take a chance on being hurt that badly again.

I meet his "I love you"s with "I know"; but as that seemed rather rude, I changed it to, "Me too." Sometimes I take his calls; most times I don't. I never return his messages, don't open his cards, and I would just as easily not go to dinner with him and instead spend the night home, alone, chatting with friends, ordering pizza, and playing poker while giving him the "I've got plans" routine.

He doesn't know me, doesn't share my dreams, and to the best of my knowledge I've never written him a single word. Come to think of it, nor have allowed him to read anything I've written or written anything in his presence. Yes, quite the change from my relationship with Jacob where he was my inspiration, my muse, my sounding board and my staunch supporter.

I don't see the hand of G-d in our ... relationship, if that is truly what it can be called. Yes, he calls when he says he's going to, arrives early to every event, dresses right for any and all occasions, and makes it well known that there is no other in his life but me. He is honest and trustworthy and everything Jacob wasn't; and I meet this with being just as distance as Jacob was to me.

Funny thing is he's not *in* my life. I don't take his advice, rarely if ever ask his opinion, and am almost offended when he offers it. I don't MAKE time for him for it is only if I have nothing better to do that I will even see him. Quite simply, he's just the guy I go to Shabbat dinner with after services on Friday night, to the social affair on Saturday evenings and to his family get-togethers on Sundays. We talk about politics, cultural affairs, and worldly travels. He wants to go with me to England on Spring Break to look at a houseboat; dreams of traveling with me this summer to Israel; and is more than willing to help me get my PhD this fall. Yes, he's everything everyone tells me I deserve in a mate.

But, I don't love him and I'm certainly not in love with him. I went down that road before with Jacob and am still carrying the pain of being discarded. I have succeeded in being strong against him, as Jacob was to me. I just don't care and maybe that is a good thing but I doubt it.

There has been no one for me for over two years; since Jacob left without so much as a good bye. I know he's moved on, found a new home, a new job, a new love. I guess those are good things if they were worth the price of losing his old home, his business, and ... me. I'd like to believe they were; that his new life is better than his old; that what he's found is better than what he, what we, had. I'd like to say I'm happy for him; but I'm not, not really. We were more than I ever hoped to find; and he threw us away for reasons I still don't understand. I guess some hurts really don't ever heal; they are just too deep.

I realize there will be a time, and not too far away, when this new guy will get tired of waiting and he'll leave or I'll just get tired of him intruding on my time and I will. I'll be good either way.

So as I readied for Temple tonight I packed up the books I needed to return to the library, the sodas for the food pantry, and the sweatshirt Jacob gave me the last time he was at my house. The poor shirt had made the rounds from lying gingerly on the bed where he used to lay, to the foot of the parlor bed where my cat used it as a comfort, to the bottom of a drawer in my closet. I guess it was time someone else got some use out of it.

His shirt was the last of the mementos, odd that I only wore it once; it was the last sign that he was ever in my life. I didn't cry as I dumped it into the bin. I find I don't do that much anymore either, it's just not worth the time and energy.

There are a lot of things I don't do anymore. I don't wish for second chances; I don't long for what was; I don't let my self be reminded of the little things, the everyday things that we did together. Perhaps that is just as well too. I have changed and I'm not all that sure it is a good thing.

I believe this new guy is a diversion; something to occupy my time when I've nothing better to do; something to help me forget; something to give me comfort in the middle of the night when I still call out ... another's name.

It isn't working.

SUMMARY

Did you see a parallel to an issue in your own life? The following ten questions may help you gain new perspective on how to manage it.

Questions to ponder:

1. Is this issue bigger than me?

2. What is my part in resolving the issue?

3. Is now the right time?

4. What's stopping me?

5. How do I remove the barriers?

6. What resources will I need to get started?

7. What resources do I have?

Answers to Act on:

8. What isn't working?

9. What is working?

10. What's the next step?

To do List:

Step 12

CLOSING NOTES

For 28 months, I waited for Jacob to come back ... or to finally say good bye. On my birthday I received an email that said ... this is the goodbye you have been asking for. He didn't actually send it to me; he sent it to an editor of mine.

I didn't cry when I read it; though it saddened me to realize it seemed that for him, nothing had changed. Where every aspect of my life had changed, he still sounded like the closet alcoholic; the controller, the manipulator, the man of idle threats and pompous arrogance.

I learned a new definition of forgiveness from a friend of mine. It was the greatest gift she'd ever given me. Her definition is: "I give up my right to be angry at you for hurting me." With this in mind I forgive Jacob.

I can't say that I know how this will truly end; for I don't. I just know that I saw the right hand of the Almighty every step of the way; and as He has asked me to do, I still wait. I don't wait as my world crashes around me; no, I take very good care of myself as I can. I don't let go undone what needs to be done, I do it. I do for others that which they cannot do for themselves and accept their help to do for me that which I cannot do for myself.

Yet, I can't imagine how life would have been if Jacob had stayed. It scares me too much. For as much as his absence hurt, I can't help but believe the Almighty saved me from a worse pain – him staying. I truly pray that the Almighty is gracious to Jacob and that He gives Jacob all the happiness he deserves.

My thanks also to *Alcoholics Anonymous* who allowed me to use their steps for the format of this work. To find a local meeting or to learn more about them, please visit their website: www.aa.org.

Feel free to contact me at: cris_robins@hotmail.com with your comments, feedback, or questions. I look forward to hearing from you.

With grace,
Ms. Christopher J. Robins

www.ingramcontent.com/pod-product-compliance
Lightning Source LLC
Chambersburg PA
CBHW061143040426
42445CB00013B/1533

9781893892040